GOD'S WORD REAL HOPE

GOD'S WORD: REAL HOPE
Copyright 1997 by God's Word to the Nations Bible Society.

GOD'S WORD **SERIES** and its associated logo are trademarks of God's Word to the Nations Bible Society.

Up to 500 verses from *GOD'S WORD* may be quoted in any form (printed, written, visual, electronic, or audio) without written permission, provided that no more than half of any one book is quoted, and the verses quoted do not amount to more than 25% of the text of the work in which they are quoted.

For quotations of over 500 verses and/or questions about these policies, please contact God's Word to the Nations Bible Society, P.O. Box 26343, Cleveland, Ohio 44126-0343, U.S.A.

Life Track notes taken from *GOD'S WORD for Students*.
Copyright 1996 by World Publishing, Inc. All rights reserved.
Used by permission of World Publishing, Inc.

Published by God's Word to the Nations Bible Society.

Printed in the United States of America.

ISBN 1-880189-15-1

Contents

REAL HOPE for a Troubled World! — v

REAL HOPE—Knowing What God Thinks About You! — vii

Now That You Have REAL HOPE . . . What Does God Want You to Do? — xv

GOD'S WORD of REAL HOPE as Told by the Apostle John — 1

A Guide to REAL HOPE — 67

REAL HOPE and Prayer — 69

REAL HOPE in the Psalms — 71

About God's Word to the Nations Bible Society — 80

REAL HOPE for a Troubled World!

The purpose of God's life-saving, life-changing message—so plainly revealed in John's account of Jesus' ministry—is clear: "These miracles have been written so that you will believe that Jesus is the Messiah, the Son of God, and so that you will have life by believing in him" (John 20:31).

Believing this sensational news provides you with *real hope* in this troubled and complex world. As Jesus says, "I've told you this so that my peace will be with you. In the world you'll have trouble. But cheer up! I have overcome the world" (John 16:33).

The world, of course, attempts to establish peace by eliminating the *external* problems that cause distress and anxiety. Jesus Christ promises, however, to provide *internal* peace to everyone who believes in him in spite of the *external* problems that trouble them. By trusting in him—even though you may be surrounded by trouble and uncertainty—you can have *real* peace of mind!

John's account in the New Testament portion of the Bible is only a small part of God's word. One of the beauties of John's particular writing is that it clearly illustrates God's plan to save you and answers some of the most common questions about Jesus:

	Chapter:Verse	Page
Why was this book written?	20:31	62
Who is Jesus?	1:29	3
Why did Jesus come into the world?	3:16-17	7

	Chapter:Verse	Page
Who will receive God's approval?	5:24	14
	6:37,40	18
What are the results of believing in Jesus?	3:16-18	7
	3:36	9
What are the results of not believing in Jesus?	3:16-19	7
	3:36	9
What did Jesus do for you?	10:11,14-15	32
What can you be sure of if you believe in Jesus?	10:27-30	33

Trust in Jesus Christ and his promise: "I'm leaving you peace. I'm giving you my peace. I don't give you the kind of peace that the world gives. So don't be troubled " (John 14:27).

In fact, please take a few minutes right now, turn to page 7, and read the *bold* text. These verses will show you the importance of believing in Jesus!

REAL HOPE— Knowing What God Thinks About You!

If you're like most people, you're very concerned about what other people think of you. You hope that others think of you as successful, thoughtful, attractive, etc. You hope that people like you.

In reality, you should be far more concerned about what God thinks of you. So, take a few moments and ask yourself the following important questions:

What does God think about you?

How can you be sure?

What does God think about you?

The following concepts based on God's revelation—as recorded in the Bible—will help you understand what God thinks about you and other humans.

Originally, humans were created good.

Then God said, "Let us make humans in our image, in our likeness...." So God created humans in his image.... He created them male and female. And God saw everything that he had made and that it was very good.

(Genesis 1:26-27,31)

Then, sin spoiled everything! As a result, our natural human condition isn't good anymore—it's corrupted. In other words, we have a problem!

The world was corrupt in God's sight and full of violence.
(Genesis 6:11)

The Lord saw how evil humans had become on the earth. All day long their deepest thoughts were nothing but evil.
(Genesis 6:5)

Indeed, I was born guilty.
I was a sinner when my mother conceived me.
(Psalm 51:5)

Not one person has God's approval.
No one has understanding.
No one searches for God.
Everyone has turned away.
Together they have become rotten to the core.
No one does anything good,
not even one person.
(Romans 3:10-12)

The consequences of this problem—our corrupted human condition—are not good!

We did what our corrupt desires and thoughts wanted us to do. So, because of our nature, we deserved God's anger just like everyone else.
(Ephesians 2:3)

People have no excuse. They knew God but did not praise and thank him for being God. Instead, their thoughts were total nonsense, and their misguided minds were plunged into darkness. While claiming to be wise, they became fools. They exchanged the glory of the immortal God for statues that looked like mortal humans, birds, animals, and snakes.

And because they thought it was worthless to acknowledge God, God allowed their own immoral minds to control them. So they do these indecent things. Their lives are filled with all kinds of sexual sins, wickedness, and greed. They are mean. They are filled with envy, murder, quarreling, deceit, and viciousness. They are gossips, slanderers, haters of God, haughty, arrogant, and boastful. They think up new ways to be cruel. They don't obey their parents, don't have any sense, don't keep promises, and don't show love to their own families or mercy to others. Although they know God's judgment that those who do such things deserve to die, they not only do these things but also approve of others who do them.

(Romans 1:20-23, 28-32)

This is a real problem because as a sinner you're separated from God. As a sinner you are condemned by God.

But your wrongs have separated you from your God,
    and your sins have made him hide his face
        so that he doesn't hear you.

(Isaiah 59:2)

The reward for sin is death . . .

(Romans 6:23)

Remember, God created us in his image. But sin spoiled everything! As a result, we don't look like God anymore.

Because all people have sinned, they have fallen short of God's glory.

(Romans 3:23)

But God wants us to look like him. In fact, he requires us to be like him.

> . . . Be holy because I, the LORD your God, am holy.
> *(Leviticus 19:2)*

However, if you believe that Jesus Christ died for you—as your substitute—on the cross, you are not condemned by God!

> God sent his Son into the world, not to condemn the world, but to save the world. Those who believe in him won't be condemned.
> *(John 3:17-18)*

> Once you were separated from God. . . . But now Christ has brought you back to God by dying in his physical body. He did this so that you could come into God's presence without sin, fault, or blame.
> *(Colossians 1:21-22)*

> The reward for sin is death, but the gift that God freely gives is everlasting life found in Christ Jesus our Lord.
> *(Romans 6:23)*

> So those who are believers in Christ Jesus can no longer be condemned.
> *(Romans 8:1)*

> God had Christ, who was sinless, take our sin so that we might receive God's approval through him.
> *(2 Corinthians 5:21)*

In other words, Jesus has taken care of the problem!

We were dead because of our failures, but he made us alive together with Christ. (It is God's kindness that saved you.) God has brought us back to life together with Christ Jesus and has given us a position in heaven with him. He did this through Christ Jesus out of his generosity to us in order to show his extremely rich kindness in the world to come. God saved you through faith as an act of kindness. You had nothing to do with it. Being saved is a gift from God. It's not the result of anything you've done, so no one can brag about it.
(Ephesians 2:5-9)

But now through Christ Jesus you, who were once far away, have been brought near by the blood of Christ.
(Ephesians 2:13)

Indeed, we, too, were once stupid, disobedient, and misled. We were slaves to many kinds of lusts and pleasures. We were mean and jealous. We were hated, and we hated each other. However, when God our Savior made his kindness and love for humanity appear, he saved us, but not because of anything we had done to gain his approval. Instead, because of his mercy he saved us through the washing in which the Holy Spirit gives us new birth and renewal. God poured a generous amount of the Spirit on us through Jesus Christ our Savior. As a result, God in his kindness has given us his approval and we have become heirs who have the confidence that we have everlasting life.
(Titus 3:3-7)

Because Jesus Christ died for you, God thinks of you as a new person.

In fact, by believing in Jesus you become a new person with the power to overcome sin and live a life that pleases God!

Whoever is a believer in Christ is a new creation. The old way of living has disappeared. A new way of living has come into existence. God has done all this. He has restored our relationship with him through Christ . . . . In other words, God was using Christ to restore his relationship with humanity. He didn't hold people's faults against them, and he has given us this message of restored relationships to tell others. Therefore, we are Christ's representatives, and through us God is calling you. We beg you on behalf of Christ to become reunited with God. God had Christ, who was sinless, take our sin so that we might receive God's approval through him.
(2 Corinthians 5:17-21)

You were also taught to become a new person created to be like God, truly righteous and holy.
(Ephesians 4:24)

Imitate God, since you are the children he loves. Live in love as Christ also loved us. He gave his life for us as an offering and sacrifice. . . .
Determine which things please the Lord. Have nothing to do with the useless works that darkness produces. . . .
(Ephesians 5:1-2, 10-11)

How can you be sure God loves you?

God says he loves you. But, how can you be sure that an unseen God really loves you?

The following passages from the Bible—God's inspired word—reveal God's unconditional love for you!

God loved the world this way: He gave his only Son so that everyone who believes in him will not die but will have eternal life.
(John 3:16)

Look at it this way: At the right time, while we were still helpless, Christ died for ungodly people. Finding someone who would die for a godly person is rare. Maybe someone would have the courage to die for a good person. Christ died for us while we were still sinners. This demonstrates God's love for us.
(Romans 5:6-8)

God didn't spare his own Son but handed him over to death for all of us. So he will also give us everything along with him.
(Romans 8:32)

So, now you know what God thinks of you!

I'm not ashamed of the Good News, It is God's power to save everyone who believes . . .
(Romans 1:16)

You heard and believed the message of truth, the Good News that he [Christ] has saved you.
(Ephesians 1:13)

These verses represent only a few of the passages in the Bible that tell you what God thinks of you and how you can be sure.

Take a few moments right now to thank God for revealing to you what he thinks of you and for proving how much he loves you by sending his only Son to die for you.

In fact, you can thank God for giving you *real hope*—now and forever—by praying:

Heavenly Father, I believe, but help my lack of faith. Help my faith to grow stronger so that I can be sure that you love me.

Thank you for revealing to me that your Son is my Savior. Thank you for demonstrating how much you love me by sending your Son, Jesus, to die for me—for my sins and failures—on the cross. Thank you for telling me that I am no longer separated from you and condemned. Now I can be sure that whenever I die I will live with you forever in heaven.

Help me—through the power of the Holy Spirit—to overcome my sins and failures. Help me to change the way I think and act and live a new life that pleases you. Help me to seek your will for my life. Help me to serve others so that other people come to know you as their Savior and Lord through me.

This prayer is offered in the name of Jesus—the One who gives me *real hope* and makes me sure! Amen!

Now That You Have REAL HOPE... What Does God Want You to Do?

First, God wants you to spread this message of hope!

God wants you to reach out to others with this message of *real hope*! The apostle Peter writes, "You are chosen people, a royal priesthood, a holy nation, people who belong to God. You were chosen to tell about the excellent qualities of God, who called you out of darkness into his marvelous light. Once you were not God's people, but now you are..." (1 Peter 2:9-10).

God expects you to tell others about your *real hope*—your faith—in Jesus Christ.

Second, God wants you to serve others!

As the apostle Paul writes, "Brothers and sisters, because of God's compassion toward us, I encourage you to offer your bodies as living sacrifices, dedicated to God and pleasing to him.... Then you will always be able to determine what God really wants—what is good, pleasing, and perfect" (Romans 12:1-2).

Through the power of the Holy Spirit you can live a life that pleases God (Philippians 1:6) by serving his people.

The apostle Paul reveals, "God has made us what we are. He has created us in Christ Jesus to live lives filled with good works that he has prepared for us to do" (Ephesians 2:10).

Remember, although good works do not save people, people who believe in Jesus—who have *real hope*—do good works that serve God's people.

John

The Word Becomes Human

¹ In the beginning the Word already existed. The Word was with God, and the Word was God. ² He was already with God in the beginning.

³ Everything came into existence through him. Not one thing that exists was made without him.

⁴ He was the source of life, and that life was the light for humanity.

⁵ The light shines in the dark, and the dark has never extinguished it.

⁶ God sent a man named John to be his messenger. ⁷ John came to declare the truth about the light so that everyone would become believers through his message. ⁸ John was not the light, but he came to declare the truth about the light.

⁹ The real light, which shines on everyone, was coming into the world. ¹⁰ He was in the world, and the world came into existence through him. Yet, the world didn't recognize him. ¹¹ He went to his own people, and his own people didn't accept him. ¹² However, he gave the right to become God's children to everyone who

---

JESUS CHRIST

Where was Jesus before he was born in Bethlehem? What did he do before he came down to earth? The apostle John clues us in to Jesus' whereabouts in the first chapter of the Gospel of John. John explains that Jesus was with God in the beginning of time. John calls Jesus "the Word," and he says that "the Word was God." He goes on to explain how Jesus was intimately involved with the whole creation of the world. See for yourself in John 1:1-3.

For more on
JESUS CHRIST,
see page 25

believed in him. ¹³ These people didn't become God's children in a physical way—from a human impulse or from a husband's desire ⌊to have a child⌋. They were born from God.

¹⁴ The Word became human and lived among us. We saw his glory. It was the glory that the Father shares with his only Son, a glory full of kindness and truth.

¹⁵ (John declared the truth about him when he said loudly, "This is the person about whom I said, 'The one who comes after me was before me because he existed before I did.'")

¹⁶ Each of us has received one gift after another because of all that the Word is. ¹⁷ The Teachings were given through Moses, but kindness and truth came into existence through Jesus Christ. ¹⁸ No one has ever seen God. God's only Son, the one who is closest to the Father's heart, has made him known.

John Prepares the Way

¹⁹ This was John's answer when the Jews sent priests and Levites from Jerusalem to ask him, "Who are you?" ²⁰ John didn't refuse to answer. He told them clearly, "I'm not the Messiah."

²¹ They asked him, "Well, are you Elijah?"

John answered, "No, I'm not."

Then they asked, "Are you the prophet?"

John replied, "No."

²² So they asked him, "Who are you? Tell us so that we can take an answer back to those who sent us. What do you say about yourself?"

²³ John said, "I'm a voice crying out in the desert, 'Make the way for the Lord straight,' as the prophet Isaiah said."

²⁴ Some of those who had been sent were Pharisees. ²⁵ They asked John, "Why do you baptize if you're not the Messiah or Elijah or the prophet?"

26 John answered them, "I baptize with water. Someone you don't know is standing among you. 27 He's the one who comes after me. I am not worthy to untie his sandal strap."

28 This happened in Bethany on the east side of the Jordan River, where John was baptizing.

John Identifies Jesus as the Lamb of God

29 *John saw Jesus coming toward him the next day and said, "Look! This is the Lamb of God who takes away the sin of the world.* 30 He is the one I spoke about when I said, 'A man who comes after me was before me because he existed before I did.' 31 I didn't know who he was. However, I came to baptize with water to show him to the people of Israel."

32 John said, "I saw the Spirit come down as a dove from heaven and stay on him. 33 I didn't know who he was. But God, who sent me to baptize with water, had told me, 'When you see the Spirit come down and stay on someone, you'll know that person is the one who baptizes with the Holy Spirit.' 34 I have seen this and have declared that this is the Son of God."

Calling of the First Disciples

35 The next day John was standing with two of his disciples. 36 John saw Jesus walk by. John said, "Look! This is the Lamb of God." 37 When the two disciples heard John say this, they followed Jesus.

38 Jesus turned around and saw them following him. He asked them, "What are you looking for?"

They said to him, "Rabbi" (which means "teacher"), "where are you staying?"

39 Jesus told them, "Come, and you will see." So they went to see where he was staying and spent the rest of that day with him. It was about ten o'clock in the morning.

⁴⁰ Andrew, Simon Peter's brother, was one of the two disciples who heard John and followed Jesus. ⁴¹ Andrew at once found his brother Simon and told him, "We have found the Messiah" (which means "Christ"). ⁴² Andrew brought Simon to Jesus.

Jesus looked at Simon and said, "You are Simon, son of John. Your name will be Cephas" (which means "Peter").

⁴³ The next day Jesus wanted to go to Galilee. He found Philip and told him, "Follow me!" ⁴⁴ (Philip was from Bethsaida, the hometown of Andrew and Peter.)

⁴⁵ Philip found Nathanael and told him, "We have found the man whom Moses wrote about in his teachings and whom the prophets wrote about. He is Jesus, son of Joseph, from the city of Nazareth."

⁴⁶ Nathanael said to Philip, "Can anything good come from Nazareth?"

Philip told him, "Come and see!"

⁴⁷ Jesus saw Nathanael coming toward him and remarked, "Here is a true Israelite who is sincere."

⁴⁸ Nathanael asked Jesus, "How do you know anything about me?"

Jesus answered him, "I saw you under the fig tree before Philip called you."

⁴⁹ Nathanael said to Jesus, "Rabbi, you are the Son of God! You are the king of Israel!"

⁵⁰ Jesus replied, "You believe because I told you that I saw you under the fig tree. You will see greater things than that." ⁵¹ Jesus said to Nathanael, "I can guarantee this truth: You will see the sky open and God's angels going up and coming down to the Son of Man."

Jesus Changes Water Into Wine

¹ Three days later a wedding took place in the city of Cana in Galilee. Jesus' mother was there. ² Jesus and his disciples had been invited too.

³ When the wine was gone, Jesus' mother said to him, "They're out of wine."

⁴ Jesus said to her, "Why did you come to me? My time has not yet come."

⁵ His mother told the servers, "Do whatever he tells you."

⁶ Six stone water jars were there. They were used for Jewish purification rituals. Each jar held 18 to 27 gallons.

⁷ Jesus told the servers, "Fill the jars with water." The servers filled the jars to the brim. ⁸ Jesus said to them, "Pour some, and take it to the person in charge." The servers did as they were told.

⁹ The person in charge tasted the water that had become wine. He didn't know where it had come from, although the servers who had poured the water knew. The person in charge called the groom ¹⁰ and said to him, "Everyone serves the best wine first. When people are drunk, the host serves cheap wine. But you have saved the best wine for now."

¹¹ Cana in Galilee was the place where Jesus began to perform miracles. He made his glory public there, and his disciples believed in him.

¹² After this, Jesus, his mother, brothers, and disciples went to the city of Capernaum and stayed there for a few days.

Jesus Throws Merchants and Moneychangers Out of the Temple Courtyard

¹³ The Jewish Passover was near, so Jesus went to Jerusalem. ¹⁴ He found those who were selling cattle, sheep, and pigeons in the temple courtyard. He also found moneychangers sitting there. ¹⁵ He made a whip from small ropes and threw everyone with their sheep and cattle out of the temple courtyard. He dumped the moneychangers' coins and knocked over their tables.

[16] He told those who sold pigeons, "Pick up this stuff, and get it out of here! Stop making my Father's house a marketplace!"

[17] His disciples remembered that Scripture said, "Devotion for your house will consume me."

[18] The Jews reacted by asking Jesus, "What miracle can you show us to justify what you're doing?"

[19] Jesus replied, "Tear down this temple, and I'll rebuild it in three days."

[20] The Jews said, "It took forty-six years to build this temple. Do you really think you're going to rebuild it in three days?"

[21] But the temple Jesus spoke about was his own body. [22] After he came back to life, his disciples remembered that he had said this. So they believed the Scripture and this statement that Jesus had made.

> **ETERNAL LIFE**
>
> Who can have eternal life? Is everyone automatically going to live forever? Everyone dies, but who gets to live on? John 3:15-18 says that everyone will NOT live forever, but that anyone who believes that Jesus is God will have eternal life. Unfortunately, everyone will not automatically have eternal life—but anyone who believes can have this gift. (Read John 3 to understand more of what it means to believe in Jesus.)

[23] While Jesus was in Jerusalem at the Passover festival, many people believed in him because they saw the miracles that he performed. [24] Jesus, however, was wary of these believers. He understood people [25] and didn't need anyone to tell him about human nature. He knew what people were really like.

A Conversation With Nicodemus

[1] Nicodemus was a Pharisee and a member of the Jewish council. [2] He came to Jesus one night and said to him, "Rabbi, we know that God has sent you as a teacher. No

one can perform the miracles you perform unless God is with him."

³ Jesus replied to Nicodemus, "I can guarantee this truth: No one can see the kingdom of God without being born from above."

⁴ Nicodemus asked him, "How can anyone be born when he's an old man? He can't go back inside his mother a second time to be born, can he?"

⁵ Jesus answered Nicodemus, "I can guarantee this truth: No one can enter the kingdom of God without being born of water and the Spirit. ⁶ Flesh and blood give birth to flesh and blood, but the Spirit gives birth to things that are spiritual. ⁷ Don't be surprised when I tell you that all of you must be born from above. ⁸ The wind blows wherever it pleases. You hear its sound, but you don't know where the wind comes from or where it's going. That's the way it is with everyone born of the Spirit."

⁹ Nicodemus replied, "How can that be?"

¹⁰ Jesus told Nicodemus, "You're a well-known teacher of Israel. Can't you understand this? ¹¹ I can guarantee this truth: We know what we're talking about, and we confirm what we've seen. Yet, you don't accept our message. ¹² If you don't believe me when I tell you about things on earth, how will you believe me when I tell you about things in heaven? ¹³ No one has gone to heaven except the Son of Man, who came from heaven.

¹⁴ "As Moses lifted up the snake [on a pole] in the desert, so the Son of Man must be lifted up. ¹⁵ Then everyone who believes in him will have eternal life."

¹⁶ *God loved the world this way: He gave his only Son so that everyone who believes in him will not die but will have eternal life. ¹⁷ God sent his Son into the world, not to condemn the world, but to save the world. ¹⁸ Those who believe in him won't be condemned. (Turn to page 9.) But those who don't*

believe are already condemned because they don't believe in God's only Son.

[19] *This is why people are condemned: The light came into the world. Yet, people loved the dark rather than the light because their actions were evil.* [20] People who do what is wrong hate the light and don't come to the light. They don't want their actions to be exposed. [21] But people who do what is true come to the light so that the things they do for God may be clearly seen.

John the Baptizer Talks About Christ

[22] Later, Jesus and his disciples went to the Judean countryside, where he spent some time with them and baptized people. [23] John was baptizing in Aenon, near Salim. Water was plentiful there. (People came to John to be baptized, [24] since John had not yet been put in prison.)

[25] Some of John's disciples had an argument with a Jew about purification ceremonies. [26] So they went to John and asked him, "Rabbi, do you remember the man you spoke so favorably about when he was with you on the other side of the Jordan River? Well, he's baptizing, and everyone is going to him!"

[27] John answered, "People can't receive anything unless it has been given to them from heaven. [28] You are witnesses that I said, 'I'm not the Messiah, but I've been sent ahead of him.'

[29] "The groom is the person to whom the bride belongs. The best man, who stands and listens to him, is overjoyed when the groom speaks. This is the joy that I feel. [30] He must increase in importance, while I must decrease in importance.

[31] "The person who comes from above is superior to everyone. I, a person from the earth, know nothing but what is on earth, and that's all I can talk about. The person who comes from heaven is superior to everyone [32] and tells what he has seen and heard. Yet, no one accepts what he

says. ³³ I have accepted what that person said, and I have affirmed that God is truthful. ³⁴The man whom God has sent speaks God's message. After all, God gives him the Spirit without limit. ³⁵ The Father loves his Son and has put everything in his power. ³⁶ *Whoever believes in the Son has eternal life, (Turn to page 14) but whoever rejects the Son will not see life. Instead, he will see God's constant anger."*

A Samaritan Woman Meets Jesus at a Well

¹ Jesus knew that the Pharisees had heard that he was making and baptizing more disciples than John. ² (Actually, Jesus was not baptizing people. His disciples were.) ³ So he left the Judean countryside and went back to Galilee.

⁴ Jesus had to go through Samaria. ⁵ He arrived at a city in Samaria called Sychar. Sychar was near the piece of land that Jacob had given to his son Joseph. ⁶ Jacob's Well was there. Jesus sat down by the well because he was tired from traveling. The time was about six o'clock in the evening.

⁷ A Samaritan woman went to get some water. Jesus said to her, "Give me a drink of water." ⁸ (His disciples had gone into the city to buy some food.)

⁹ The Samaritan woman asked him, "How can a Jewish man like you ask a Samaritan woman like me for a drink of water?" (Jews, of course, don't associate with Samaritans.)

¹⁰ Jesus replied to her, "If you only knew what God's gift is and who is asking you for a drink, you would have asked him for a drink. He would have given you living water."

¹¹ The woman said to him, "Sir, you don't have anything to use to get water, and the well is deep. So where are you going to get this living water? ¹² You're not more important than our ancestor Jacob, are you? He

gave us this well. He and his sons and his animals drank water from it."

[13] Jesus answered her, "Everyone who drinks this water will become thirsty again. [14] But those who drink the water that I will give them will never become thirsty again. In fact, the water I will give them will become in them a spring that gushes up to eternal life."

[15] The woman told Jesus, "Sir, give me this water! Then I won't get thirsty or have to come here to get water."

[16] Jesus told her, "Go to your husband, and bring him here."

[17] The woman replied, "I don't have a husband."

Jesus told her, "You're right when you say that you don't have a husband. [18] You've had five husbands, and the man you have now isn't your husband. You've told the truth."

[19] The woman said to Jesus, "I see that you're a prophet! [20] Our ancestors worshiped on this mountain. But you Jews say that people must worship in Jerusalem."

[21] Jesus told her, "Believe me. A time is coming when you Samaritans won't be worshiping the Father on this mountain or in Jerusalem. [22] You don't know what you're worshiping. We ⌊Jews⌋ know what we're worshiping, because salvation comes from the Jews. [23] Indeed, the time is coming, and it is now here, when the true worshipers will worship the Father in spirit and truth. The Father is looking for people like that to worship him. [24] God is a spirit. Those who worship him must worship in spirit and truth."

CHURCH

Jesus was confronted by a woman at a well, and their conversation quickly turned to spiritual matters. While the woman wanted to debate where to worship God, Jesus settled the matter by telling her that what really mattered was the condition of her heart. God is more interested in the quality and condition of our hearts than he is in the size or location of our church building. Find out what Jesus had to say to this woman in John 4:21-24.

²⁵ The woman said to him, "I know that the Messiah is coming. When he comes, he will tell us everything." (*Messiah* is the one called *Christ*.)

²⁶ Jesus told her, "I am he, and I am speaking to you now."

²⁷ At that time his disciples returned. They were surprised that he was talking to a woman. But none of them asked him, "What do you want from her?" or "Why are you talking to her?"

²⁸ Then the woman left her water jar and went back into the city. She told the people, ²⁹ "Come with me, and meet a man who told me everything I've ever done. Could he be the Messiah?" ³⁰ The people left the city and went to meet Jesus.

> **RESPONSIBILITY**
>
> Jesus used an example from agriculture to motivate us in our responsibility to witness. People all around us are ready right now to respond to the Good News about Jesus. Don't put off the responsibility of telling a close friend about Christ because it never seems to be "the right time." Jesus says that now is the right time to tell others about him. Read in John 4:4-42 about a woman who was ready to respond to Jesus.

³¹ Meanwhile, the disciples were urging him, "Rabbi, have something to eat."

³² Jesus told them, "I have food to eat that you don't know about."

³³ The disciples asked each other, "Did someone bring him something to eat?"

³⁴ Jesus told them, "My food is to do what the one who sent me wants me to do and to finish the work he has given me.

³⁵ "Don't you say, 'In four more months the harvest will be here'? I'm telling you to look and see that the fields are ready to be harvested. ³⁶ The person who harvests the crop is already getting paid. He is gathering grain for eternal life. So the person who plants the grain and the person who harvests it are happy together. ³⁷ In

this respect the saying is true: 'One person plants, and another person harvests.' ³⁸ I have sent you to harvest a crop you have not worked for. Other people have done the hard work, and you have followed them in their work."

³⁹ Many Samaritans in that city believed in Jesus because of the woman who said, "He told me everything I've ever done." ⁴⁰ So when the Samaritans went to Jesus, they asked him to stay with them. He stayed in Samaria for two days. ⁴¹ Many more Samaritans believed because of what Jesus said. ⁴² They told the woman, "Our faith is no longer based on what you've said. We have heard him ourselves, and we know that he really is the savior of the world."

A Believing Official

⁴³ After spending two days in Samaria, Jesus left for Galilee. ⁴⁴ Jesus had said that a prophet is not honored in his own country. ⁴⁵ But when Jesus arrived in Galilee, the people of Galilee welcomed him. They had seen everything he had done at the festival in Jerusalem, since they, too, had attended the festival.

⁴⁶ Jesus returned to the city of Cana in Galilee, where he had changed water into wine. A government official was in Cana. His son was sick in Capernaum. ⁴⁷ The official heard that Jesus had returned from Judea to Galilee. So he went to Jesus and asked him to go to Capernaum with him to heal his son who was about to die.

⁴⁸ Jesus told the official, "If people don't see miracles and amazing things, they won't believe."

⁴⁹ The official said to him, "Sir, come with me before my little boy dies."

⁵⁰ Jesus told him, "Go home. Your son will live." The man believed what Jesus told him and left.

⁵¹ While the official was on his way to Capernaum, his servants met him and told him that his boy was alive. ⁵² The official asked them at what time his son got better. His servants told him, "The fever left him yesterday evening at

seven o'clock." ⁵³ Then the boy's father realized that it was the same time that Jesus had told him, "Your son will live." So the official and his entire family became believers.

⁵⁴ This was the second miracle that Jesus performed after he had come back from Judea to Galilee.

Jesus Cures a Man at the Bethesda Pool

¹ Later, Jesus went to Jerusalem for a Jewish festival.

² Near Sheep Gate in Jerusalem was a pool called *Bethesda* in Hebrew. It had five porches. ³ Under these porches a large number of sick people—people who were blind, lame, or paralyzed—used to lie. ⁵ One man, who had been sick for 38 years, was lying there. ⁶ Jesus saw the man lying there and knew that he had been sick for a long time. So Jesus asked the man, "Would you like to get well?"

⁷ The sick man answered Jesus, "Sir, I don't have anyone to put me into the pool when the water is stirred. While I'm trying to get there, someone else steps into the pool ahead of me."

⁸ Jesus told the man, "Get up, pick up your cot, and walk." ⁹ The man immediately became well, picked up his cot, and walked.

That happened on a day of worship. ¹⁰ So the Jews told the man who had been healed, "This is a day of worship. You're not allowed to carry your cot today."

¹¹ The man replied, "The man who made me well told me to pick up my cot and walk."

¹² The Jews asked him, "Who is the man who told you to pick it up and walk?" ¹³ But the man who had been healed didn't know who Jesus was. (Jesus had withdrawn from the crowd.)

¹⁴ Later, Jesus met the man in the temple courtyard and told him, "You're well now. Stop sinning so that something worse doesn't happen to you."

¹⁵ The man went back to the Jews and told them that Jesus was the man who had made him well.

The Son Is Equal to the Father

¹⁶ The Jews began to persecute Jesus because he kept healing people on the day of worship. ¹⁷ Jesus replied to them, "My Father is working right now, and so am I."

¹⁸ His reply made the Jews more intent on killing him. Not only did he break the laws about the day of worship, but also he made himself equal to God when he said repeatedly that God was his Father.

¹⁹ Jesus said to the Jews, "I can guarantee this truth: The Son cannot do anything on his own. He can do only what he sees the Father doing. Indeed, the Son does exactly what the Father does. ²⁰ The Father loves the Son and shows him everything he is doing. The Father will show him even greater things to do than these things so that you will be amazed. ²¹ In the same way that the Father brings back the dead and gives them life, the Son gives life to anyone he chooses.

²² "The Father doesn't judge anyone. He has entrusted judgment entirely to the Son ²³ so that everyone will honor the Son as they honor the Father. Whoever doesn't honor the Son doesn't honor the Father who sent him. ²⁴ *I can guarantee this truth: Those who listen to what I say and believe in the one who sent me will have eternal life. They won't be judged because they have already passed from death to life. (Turn to page 18.)*

²⁵ "I can guarantee this truth: A time is coming (and is now here) when the dead will hear the voice of the Son of God and those who respond to it will live. ²⁶ The Father is the source of life, and he has enabled the Son to be the source of life too.

²⁷ "He has also given the Son authority to pass judgment because he is the Son of Man. ²⁸ Don't be surprised at what I've just said. A time is coming when all the dead will hear

his voice, [29] and they will come out of their tombs. Those who have done good will come back to life and live. But those who have done evil will come back to life and will be judged. [30] I can't do anything on my own. As I listen ⌊to the Father⌋, I make my judgments. My judgments are right because I don't try to do what I want but what the one who sent me wants.

[31] "If I testify on my own behalf, what I say isn't true. [32] Someone else testifies on my behalf, and I know that what he says about me is true. [33] You sent people to John ⌊the Baptizer⌋, and he testified to the truth. [34] But I don't depend on human testimony. I'm telling you this to save you. [35] John was a lamp that gave off brilliant light. For a time you enjoyed the pleasure of his light. [36] But I have something that testifies more favorably on my behalf than John's testimony. The tasks that the Father gave me to carry out, these tasks which I perform, testify on my behalf. They prove that the Father has sent me. [37] The Father who sent me testifies on my behalf. You have never heard his voice, and you have never seen his form. [38] So you don't have the Father's message within you, because you don't believe in the person he has sent. [39] You study the Scriptures in detail because you think you have the source of eternal life in them. These Scriptures testify on my behalf. [40] Yet, you don't want to come to me to get ⌊eternal⌋ life.

[41] "I don't accept praise from humans. [42] But I know what kind of people you are. You don't have any love for God. [43] I have come with the authority my Father has given me, but you don't accept me. If someone else comes with his own authority, you will accept him. [44] How can you believe when you accept each other's praise and don't look for the praise that comes from the only God?

[45] "Don't think that I will accuse you in the presence of the Father. Moses, the one you trust, is already accusing you. [46] If you really believed Moses, you would

believe me. Moses wrote about me. [47] If you don't believe what Moses wrote, how will you ever believe what I say?"

Jesus Feeds More Than Five Thousand

[1] Jesus later crossed to the other side of the Sea of Galilee (or the Sea of Tiberias). [2] A large crowd followed him because they saw the miracles that he performed for the sick. [3] Jesus went up a mountain and sat with his disciples. [4] The time for the Jewish Passover festival was near.

[5] As Jesus saw a large crowd coming to him, he said to Philip, "Where can we buy bread for these people to eat?" [6] Jesus asked this question to test him. He already knew what he was going to do.

[7] Philip answered, "We would need about a year's wages to buy enough bread for each of them to have a piece."

[8] One of Jesus' disciples, Andrew, who was Simon Peter's brother, told him, [9] "A boy who has five loaves of barley bread and two small fish is here. But they won't go very far for so many people."

[10] Jesus said, "Have the people sit down."

The people had plenty of grass to sit on. (There were about 5,000 men in the crowd.)

[11] Jesus took the loaves, gave thanks, and distributed them to the people who were sitting there. He did the same thing with the fish. All the people ate as much as they wanted.

[12] When the people were full, Jesus told his disciples, "Gather the leftover pieces so that nothing will be wasted." [13] The disciples gathered the leftover pieces of bread and filled twelve baskets.

[14] When the people saw the miracle Jesus performed, they said, "This man is certainly the prophet who is to come into the world." [15] Jesus realized that the people intended to take him by force and make him king. So he returned to the mountain by himself.

Jesus Walks on the Sea

[16] When evening came, his disciples went to the sea. [17] They got into a boat and started to cross the sea to the city of Capernaum. By this time it was dark, and Jesus had not yet come to them. [18] A strong wind started to blow and stir up the sea.

[19] After they had rowed three or four miles, they saw Jesus walking on the sea. He was coming near the boat, and they became terrified.

[20] Jesus told them, "It's me. Don't be afraid!"

[21] So they were willing to help Jesus into the boat. Immediately, the boat reached the shore where they were going.

Jesus Is the Bread of Life

[22] On the next day the people were still on the other side of the sea. They noticed that only one boat was there and that Jesus had not stepped into that boat with his disciples. The disciples had gone away without him. [23] Other boats from Tiberias arrived near the place where they had eaten the bread after the Lord gave thanks. [24] When the people saw that neither Jesus nor his disciples were there, they got into these boats and went to the city of Capernaum to look for Jesus. [25] When they found him on the other side of the sea, they asked him, "Rabbi, when did you get here?"

[26] Jesus replied to them, "I can guarantee this truth: You're not looking for me because you saw miracles. You are looking for me because you ate as much of those loaves as you wanted. [27] Don't work for food that spoils. Instead, work for the food that lasts into eternal life. This is the food the Son of Man will give you. After all, the Father has placed his seal of approval on him."

[28] The people asked Jesus, "What does God want us to do?"

²⁹ Jesus replied to them, "God wants to do something for you so that you believe in the one whom he has sent."

³⁰ The people asked him, "What miracle are you going to perform so that we can see it and believe in you? What are you going to do? ³¹ Our ancestors ate the manna in the desert. Scripture says, 'He gave them bread from heaven to eat.'"

³² Jesus said to them, "I can guarantee this truth: Moses didn't give you bread from heaven, but my Father gives you the true bread from heaven. ³³ God's bread is the man who comes from heaven and gives life to the world."

³⁴ They said to him, "Sir, give us this bread all the time."

³⁵ Jesus told them, "I am the bread of life. Whoever comes to me will never become hungry, and whoever believes in me will never become thirsty. ³⁶ I've told you that you have seen me. However, you don't believe in me. ³⁷ *Everyone whom the Father gives me will come to me. I will never turn away anyone who comes to me.* ³⁸ I haven't come from heaven to do what I want to do. I've come to do what the one who sent me wants me to do. ³⁹ The one who sent me doesn't want me to lose any of those he gave me. He wants me to bring them back to life on the last day. ⁴⁰ *My Father wants all those who see the Son and believe in him to have eternal life. He wants me to bring them back to life on the last day." (Turn to page 19.)*

⁴¹ The Jews began to criticize Jesus for saying, "I am the bread that came from heaven." ⁴² They asked, "Isn't this man Jesus, Joseph's son? Don't we know his father and mother? How can he say now, 'I came from heaven'?"

SELFISHNESS

Following your own way can lead you down the wrong road. Jesus, with all of heaven and earth at his command, did not demand his own way. He lived according to God's plan for his life. Read more about this plan in John 6:35-40. Choose God's way over your own desires for your life. Then get ready to experience his very best in every area of your life.

[43] Jesus responded, "Stop criticizing me! [44] People cannot come to me unless the Father who sent me brings them to me. I will bring these people back to life on the last day. [45] The prophets wrote, 'God will teach everyone.' Those who do what they have learned from the Father come to me. [46] I'm saying that no one has seen the Father. Only the one who is from God has seen the Father. [47] **I can guarantee this truth: Every believer has eternal life. (Turn to page 26.)**

[48] "I am the bread of life. [49] Your ancestors ate the manna in the desert and died. [50] This is the bread that comes from heaven so that whoever eats it won't die. [51] I am the living bread that came from heaven. Whoever eats this bread will live forever. The bread I will give to bring life to the world is my flesh."

[52] The Jews began to quarrel with each other. They said, "How can this man give us his flesh to eat?"

[53] Jesus told them, "I can guarantee this truth: If you don't eat the flesh of the Son of Man and drink his blood, you don't have the source of life in you. [54] Those who eat my flesh and drink my blood have eternal life, and I will bring them back to life on the last day. [55] My flesh is true food, and my blood is true drink. [56] Those who eat my flesh and drink my blood live in me, and I live in them.

ETERNAL LIFE

Some people might say there are many ways to go to heaven. But in John 6:69, Peter stated the fact that no one else but Christ offers any hope for eternal life. Several of Jesus' followers had decided his teachings were too hard, and they chose not to follow him any longer. (Read John 6 to see what these hard teachings were.) But when Jesus asked the rest of his followers if they would leave him, too, Peter said there was nowhere else to go—only Christ's words give eternal life. Nothing has changed since then; there is still no other way to have peace with God and live after death. Following Christ may be difficult at times, but it's the only option.

⁵⁷ The Father who has life sent me, and I live because of the Father. So those who feed on me will live because of me. ⁵⁸ This is the bread that came from heaven. It is not like the bread your ancestors ate. They eventually died. Those who eat this bread will live forever."

⁵⁹ Jesus said this while he was teaching in a synagogue in Capernaum. ⁶⁰ When many of Jesus' disciples heard him, they said, "What he says is hard to accept. Who wants to listen to him anymore?"

⁶¹ Jesus was aware that his disciples were criticizing his message. So Jesus asked them, "Did what I say make you lose faith? ⁶² What if you see the Son of Man go where he was before? ⁶³ Life is spiritual. Your physical existence doesn't contribute to that life. The words that I have spoken to you are spiritual. They are life. ⁶⁴ But some of you don't believe." Jesus knew from the beginning those who wouldn't believe and the one who would betray him. ⁶⁵ So he added, "That is why I told you that people cannot come to me unless the Father provides the way."

⁶⁶ Jesus' speech made many of his disciples go back to the lives they had led before they followed Jesus. ⁶⁷ So Jesus asked the twelve apostles, "Do you want to leave me too?"

⁶⁸ Simon Peter answered Jesus, "Lord, to what person could we go? Your words give eternal life. ⁶⁹ Besides, we believe and know that you are the Holy One of God."

⁷⁰ Jesus replied, "I chose all twelve of you. Yet, one of you is a devil." ⁷¹ Jesus meant Judas, son of Simon Iscariot. Judas, who was one of the twelve apostles, would later betray Jesus.

Jesus Goes to the Festival of Booths

¹ Jesus later traveled throughout Galilee. He didn't want to travel in Judea because Jews there wanted to kill him.

² The time for the Jewish Festival of Booths was near. ³ So Jesus' brothers told him, "Leave this place, and go to Judea so that your disciples can see the things that you're

doing. ⁴ No one does things secretly when he wants to be known publicly. If you do these things, you should let the world see you." ⁵ Even his brothers didn't believe in him.

⁶ Jesus told them, "Now is not the right time for me to go. Any time is right for you. ⁷ The world cannot hate you, but it hates me because I say that what everyone does is evil. ⁸ Go to the festival. I'm not going to this festival right now. Now is not the right time for me to go."

⁹ After saying this, Jesus stayed in Galilee. ¹⁰ But after his brothers had gone to the festival, Jesus went. He didn't go publicly but secretly.

¹¹ The Jews were looking for Jesus in the crowd at the festival. They kept asking, "Where is that man?" ¹² The crowds argued about Jesus. Some people said, "He's a good man," while others said, "No he isn't. He deceives the people." ¹³ Yet, no one would talk openly about him because they were afraid of the Jews.

¹⁴ When the festival was half over, Jesus went to the temple courtyard and began to teach. ¹⁵ The Jews were surprised and asked, "How can this man be so educated when he hasn't gone to school?"

¹⁶ Jesus responded to them, "What I teach doesn't come from me but from the one who sent me. ¹⁷ Those who want to follow the will of God will know if what I teach is from God or if I teach my own thoughts. ¹⁸ Those who speak their own thoughts are looking for their own glory. But the man who wants to bring glory to the one who sent him is a true teacher and doesn't have dishonest motives. ¹⁹ Didn't Moses give you his teachings? Yet, none of you does what Moses taught you. So why do you want to kill me?"

²⁰ The crowd answered, "You're possessed by a demon! Who wants to kill you?"

²¹ Jesus answered them, "I performed one miracle, and all of you are surprised by it. ²² Moses gave you the teaching about circumcision (although it didn't come from Moses but from our ancestors). So you circumcise a male on a day of worship. ²³ If you circumcise a male on the day of worship to follow Moses' Teachings, why are you angry with me because I made a man entirely well on the day of worship? ²⁴ Stop judging by outward appearance! Instead, judge correctly."

²⁵ Some of the people who lived in Jerusalem said, "Isn't this the man they want to kill? ²⁶ But look at this! He's speaking in public, and no one is saying anything to him! Can it be that the rulers really know that this man is the Messiah? ²⁷ However, we know where this man comes from. When the Christ comes, no one will know where he is from."

²⁸ Then, while Jesus was teaching in the temple courtyard, he said loudly, "You know me, and you know where I come from. I didn't decide to come on my own. The one who sent me is true. He's the one you don't know. ²⁹ I know him because I am from him and he sent me."

³⁰ The Jews tried to arrest him but couldn't because his time had not yet come.

³¹ However, many people in the crowd believed in him. They asked, "When the Messiah comes, will he perform more miracles than this man has?"

³² The Pharisees heard the crowd saying things like this about him. So the chief priests and the Pharisees sent temple guards to arrest Jesus.

³³ Jesus said, "I will still be with you for a little while. Then I'll go to the one who sent me. ³⁴ You will look for me, but you won't find me. You can't go where I'm going."

³⁵ The Jews said among themselves, "Where does this man intend to go so that we won't find him? Does he mean that he'll live with the Jews who are scattered among the Greeks and that he'll teach the Greeks? ³⁶ What does he

mean when he says, 'You will look for me, but you won't find me,' and 'You can't go where I'm going'?"

37 On the last and most important day of the festival, Jesus was standing ₍in the temple courtyard₎. He said loudly, "Whoever is thirsty must come to me to drink. 38 As Scripture says, 'Streams of living water will flow from deep within the person who believes in me.'" 39 Jesus said this about the Spirit, whom his believers would receive. The Spirit was not yet evident, as it would be after Jesus had been glorified.

40 After some of the crowd heard Jesus say these words, they said, "This man is certainly the prophet." 41 Other people said, "This man is the Messiah." Still other people asked, "How can the Messiah come from Galilee? 42 Doesn't Scripture say that the Messiah will come from the descendants of David and from the village of Bethlehem, where David lived?" 43 So the people were divided because of Jesus. 44 Some of them wanted to arrest him, but they couldn't.

45 When the temple guards returned, the chief priests and Pharisees asked them, "Why didn't you bring Jesus?"

46 The temple guards answered, "No human has ever spoken like this man."

47 The Pharisees asked the temple guards, "Have you been deceived too? 48 Has any ruler or any Pharisee believed in him? 49 This crowd is cursed because it doesn't know Moses' Teachings."

50 One of those Pharisees was Nicodemus, who had previously visited Jesus. Nicodemus asked them, 51 "Do Moses' Teachings enable us to judge a person without first hearing that person's side of the story? We can't judge a person without finding out what that person has done."

⁵² They asked Nicodemus, "Are you saying this because you're from Galilee? Study ⌊the Scriptures⌋, and you'll see that no prophet comes from Galilee."

⁵³ Then each of them went home.

A Woman Caught in Adultery

¹ Jesus went to the Mount of Olives. ² Early the next morning he returned to the temple courtyard. All the people went to him, so he sat down and began to teach them.

³ The scribes and the Pharisees brought a woman who had been caught committing adultery. They made her stand in front of everyone ⁴ and asked Jesus, "Teacher, we caught this woman in the act of adultery. ⁵ In his teachings, Moses ordered us to stone women like this to death. What do you say?" ⁶ They asked this to test him. They wanted to find a reason to bring charges against him.

Jesus bent down and used his finger to write on the ground. ⁷ When they persisted in asking him questions, he straightened up and said, "The person who is sinless should be the first to throw a stone at her." ⁸ Then he bent down again and continued writing on the ground.

⁹ One by one, beginning with the older men, the scribes and Pharisees left. Jesus was left alone with the woman. ¹⁰ Then Jesus straightened up and asked her, "Where did they go? Has anyone condemned you?"

¹¹ The woman answered, "No one, sir."

Jesus said, "I don't condemn you either. Go! From now on don't sin."

Jesus Speaks With the Pharisees About His Father

¹² Jesus spoke to the Pharisees again. He said, "I am the light of the world. Whoever follows me will have a life filled with light and will never live in the dark."

¹³ The Pharisees said to him, "You testify on your own behalf, so your testimony isn't true."

[14] Jesus replied to them, "Even if I testify on my own behalf, my testimony is true because I know where I came from and where I'm going. However, you don't know where I came from or where I'm going. [15] You judge the way humans do. I don't judge anyone. [16] Even if I do judge, my judgment is valid because I don't make it on my own. I make my judgment with the Father who sent me. [17] Your own teachings say that the testimony of two people is true. [18] I testify on my own behalf, and so does the Father who sent me."

> **JESUS CHRIST**
>
> Darkness makes it difficult to see where we're going. Spiritual darkness makes it impossible to know how to get to God. Through Jesus Christ, we have a solution to the problem of spiritual darkness. Because of him, we have the light we need for life. Through him, we can have a significant, meaningful relationship with God. To see how to follow in God's light, read John 8:12-59.
>
> **For more on JESUS CHRIST, see page 32.**

[19] The Pharisees asked him, "Where is your father?"

Jesus replied, "You don't know me or my Father. If you knew me, you would also know my Father."

[20] Jesus spoke these words while he was teaching in the treasury area of the temple courtyard. No one arrested him, because his time had not yet come.

[21] Jesus spoke to the Pharisees again. He said, "I'm going away, and you'll look for me. But you will die because of your sin. You can't go where I'm going."

[22] Then the Jews asked, "Is he going to kill himself? Is that what he means when he says, 'You can't go where I'm going'?"

[23] Jesus said to them, "You're from below. I'm from above. You're from this world. I'm not from this world. [24] For this reason I told you that you'll die because of your sins. If you don't believe that I am the one, you'll die because of your sins."

[25] The Jews asked him, "Who did you say you are?"

Jesus told them, "I am who I said I was from the beginning. [26] I have a lot I could say about you and a lot I could condemn you for. But the one who sent me is true. So I tell the world exactly what he has told me." [27] (The Jews didn't know that he was talking to them about the Father.)

[28] So Jesus told them, "When you have lifted up the Son of Man, then you'll know that I am the one and that I can't do anything on my own. Instead, I speak as the Father taught me. [29] Besides, the one who sent me is with me. He hasn't left me by myself. I always do what pleases him."

[30] As Jesus was saying this, many people believed in him. [31] So Jesus said to those Jews who believed in him, **"If you live by what I say, you are truly my disciples. [32] You will know the truth, and the truth will set you free."**

[33] They replied to Jesus, "We are Abraham's descendants, and we've never been anyone's slaves. So how can you say that we will be set free?"

[34] Jesus answered them, "I can guarantee this truth: Whoever lives a sinful life is a slave to sin. [35] A slave doesn't live in the home forever, but a son does. [36] **So if the Son sets you free, you will be absolutely free. (Turn to page 32.)** [37] I know that you're Abraham's descendants. However, you want to kill me because you don't like what I'm saying. [38] What I'm saying is what I have seen in my Father's presence. But you do what you've heard from your father."

[39] The Jews replied to Jesus, "Abraham is our father."

SIN

Whether you learned it in history class or from your family's own history, you know something of what slavery is like. The master determined nearly every aspect of life for his or her slaves. Jesus said to the Jews that people who sin are slaves to sin. His words are still true: Sin can run your life and make all your decisions for you—if you let it. Don't underestimate the power of sin. Read more of Jesus' conversation with the Jews about slavery and freedom in John 8:30-47.

Jesus told them, "If you were Abraham's children, you would do what Abraham did. [40] I am a man who has told you the truth that I heard from God. But now you want to kill me. Abraham wouldn't have done that. [41] You're doing what your father does."

The Jews said to Jesus, "We're not illegitimate children. God is our only Father."

[42] Jesus told them, "If God were your Father, you would love me. After all, I'm here, and I came from God. I didn't come on my own. Instead, God sent me. [43] Why don't you understand the language I use? Is it because you can't understand the words I use? [44] You come from your father, the devil, and you desire to do what your father wants you to do. The devil was a murderer from the beginning. He has never been truthful. He doesn't know what the truth is. Whenever he tells a lie, he's doing what comes naturally to him. He's a liar and the father of lies. [45] So you don't believe me because I tell the truth. [46] Can any of you convict me of committing a sin? If I'm telling the truth, why don't you believe me? [47] The person who belongs to God understands what God says. You don't understand because you don't belong to God."

[48] The Jews replied to Jesus, "Aren't we right when we say that you're a Samaritan and that you're possessed by a demon?"

[49] Jesus answered, "I'm not possessed. I honor my Father, but you dishonor me. [50] I don't want my own glory. But there is someone who wants it, and he is the judge. [51] I can guarantee this truth: Whoever obeys what I say will never see death."

[52] The Jews told Jesus, "Now we know that you're possessed by a demon. Abraham died, and so did the prophets, but you say, 'Whoever does what I say will never taste death.' [53] Are you greater than our father Abraham, who died? The prophets have also died. Who do you think you are?"

⁵⁴ Jesus said, "If I bring glory to myself, my glory is nothing. My Father is the one who gives me glory, and you say that he is your God. ⁵⁵ Yet, you haven't known him. However, I know him. If I would say that I didn't know him, I would be a liar like all of you. But I do know him, and I do what he says. ⁵⁶ Your father Abraham was pleased to see that my day was coming. He saw it and was happy."

⁵⁷ The Jews said to Jesus, "You're not even fifty years old. How could you have seen Abraham?"

⁵⁸ Jesus told them, "I can guarantee this truth: Before Abraham was ever born, I am."

⁵⁹ Then some of the Jews picked up stones to throw at Jesus. However, Jesus was concealed, and he left the temple courtyard.

Jesus Gives Sight to a Blind Man

¹ As Jesus walked along, he saw a man who had been born blind. ² His disciples asked him, "Rabbi, why was this man born blind? Did he or his parents sin?"

³ Jesus answered, "Neither this man nor his parents sinned. Instead, he was born blind so that God could show what he can do for him. ⁴ We must do what the one who sent me wants us to do while it is day. The night when no one can do anything is coming. ⁵ As long as I'm in the world, I'm light for the world."

⁶ After Jesus said this, he spit on the ground and mixed the spit with dirt. Then he smeared it on the man's eyes ⁷ and told him, "Wash it off in the pool of Siloam." (*Siloam* means "sent.") The blind man washed it off and returned. He was able to see.

⁸ His neighbors and those who had previously seen him begging asked, "Isn't this the man who used to sit and beg?"

⁹ Some of them said, "He's the one." Others said, "No, he isn't, but he looks like him." But the man himself said, "I am the one."

¹⁰ So they asked him, "How did you receive your sight?"

¹¹ He replied, "The man people call Jesus mixed some spit with dirt, smeared it on my eyes, and told me, 'Go to Siloam, and wash it off.' So I went there, washed it off, and received my sight."

¹² They asked him, "Where is that man?"

The man answered, "I don't know."

¹³ Some people brought the man who had been blind to the Pharisees. ¹⁴ The day when Jesus mixed the spit and dirt and gave the man sight was a day of worship. ¹⁵ So the Pharisees asked the man again how he received his sight.

The man told the Pharisees, "He put a mixture of spit and dirt on my eyes. I washed it off, and now I can see."

¹⁶ Some of the Pharisees said, "The man who did this is not from God because he doesn't follow the traditions for the day of worship." Other Pharisees asked, "How can a man who is a sinner perform miracles like these?" So the Pharisees were divided in their opinions.

¹⁷ They asked the man who had been born blind another question: "What do you say about the man who gave you sight?"

The man answered, "He's a prophet."

¹⁸ Until they talked to the man's parents, the Jews didn't believe that the man had been blind and had been given sight. ¹⁹ They asked his parents, "Is this your son, the one you say was born blind? Why can he see now?"

²⁰ His parents replied, "We know that he's our son and that he was born blind. ²¹ But we don't know how he got his sight or who gave it to him. You'll have to ask him. He's old enough to answer for himself." ²² (His parents said this because they were afraid of the Jews. The Jews had already agreed to put anyone who acknowledged that Jesus was the Christ out of the synagogue. ²³ That's

why his parents said, "You'll have to ask him. He's old enough.")

²⁴ So once again the Jews called the man who had been blind. They told him, "Give glory to God. We know that this man who gave you sight is a sinner."

²⁵ The man responded, "I don't know if he's a sinner or not. But I do know one thing. I used to be blind, but now I can see."

²⁶ The Jews asked him, "What did he do to you? How did he give you sight?"

²⁷ The man replied, "I've already told you, but you didn't listen. Why do you want to hear the story again? Do you want to become his disciples too?"

²⁸ The Jews yelled at him, "You're his disciple, but we're Moses' disciples. ²⁹ We know that God spoke to Moses, but we don't know where this man came from."

³⁰ The man replied to them, "That's amazing! You don't know where he's from. Yet, he gave me sight. ³¹ We know that God doesn't listen to sinners. Instead, he listens to people who are devout and who do what he wants. ³² Since the beginning of time, no one has ever heard of anyone giving sight to a person born blind. ³³ If this man were not from God, he couldn't do anything like that."

³⁴ The Jews answered him, "You were born full of sin. Do you think you can teach us?" Then they threw him out ⌊of the synagogue⌋.

³⁵ Jesus heard that the Jews had thrown the man out ⌊of the synagogue⌋. So when Jesus found the man, he asked him, "Do you believe in the Son of Man?"

³⁶ The man replied, "Sir, tell me who he is so that I can believe in him."

³⁷ Jesus told him, "You've seen him. He is the person who is now talking with you."

³⁸ The man bowed in front of Jesus and said, "I believe, Lord."

³⁹ Then Jesus said, "I have come into this world to judge: Blind people will be given sight, and those who can see will become blind."

⁴⁰ Some Pharisees who were with Jesus heard this. So they asked him, "Do you think we're blind?"

⁴¹ Jesus told them, "If you were blind, you wouldn't be sinners. But now you say, 'We see,' so you continue to be sinners.

> **GUILT**
>
> Sin has an amazing way of blinding us to our guilt. The Pharisees were religious leaders who refused to see their own spiritual blindness. Their hypocrisy caused them to believe that they were OK when they were really quite sinful. Be careful that you don't overlook your sin and falsely believe that you are free from guilt. Learn what Jesus told the Pharisees in John 9:41.

Jesus, the Good Shepherd

¹ "I can guarantee this truth: The person who doesn't enter the sheep pen through the gate but climbs in somewhere else is a thief or a robber. ² But the one who enters through the gate is the shepherd. ³ The gatekeeper opens the gate for him, and the sheep respond to his voice. He calls his sheep by name and leads them out of the pen. ⁴ After he has brought out all his sheep, he walks ahead of them. The sheep follow him because they recognize his voice. ⁵ They won't follow a stranger. Instead, they will run away from a stranger because they don't recognize his voice." ⁶ Jesus used this illustration as he talked to the people, but they didn't understand what he meant.

⁷ Jesus emphasized, "I can guarantee this truth: I am the gate for the sheep. ⁸ All who came before I did were thieves or robbers. However, the sheep didn't respond to them. ⁹ I am the gate. Those who enter the sheep pen through me will be saved. They will go in and out of the sheep pen and find food. ¹⁰ A thief comes to steal, kill, and destroy. But I came so that my sheep will have life and so that they will have everything they need.

> **JESUS CHRIST**
> Getting locked out of your house is frustrating. You have to wait for help in order to get inside. In John 10, Jesus provides assistance when we are spiritually "locked out." Jesus said that he is the gate and whoever enters into a relationship with God through him will be saved. Jesus promised never to lock us out. He promised to allow us to develop a relationship with him. Check out the open gate in John 10:9

[11] *"I am the good shepherd. The good shepherd gives his life for the sheep.* [12] A hired hand isn't a shepherd and doesn't own the sheep. When he sees a wolf coming, he abandons the sheep and quickly runs away. So the wolf drags the sheep away and scatters the flock. [13] The hired hand is concerned about what he's going to get paid and not about the sheep.

[14] *"I am the good shepherd. I know my sheep as the Father knows me. My sheep know me as I know the Father.* [15] *So I give my life for my sheep.* **(Turn to page 33.)** [16] I also have other sheep that are not from this pen. I must lead them. They, too, will respond to my voice. So they will be one flock with one shepherd. [17] The Father loves me because I give my life in order to take it back again. [18] No one takes my life from me. I give my life of my own free will. I have the authority to give my life, and I have the authority to take my life back again. This is what my Father ordered me to do."

[19] The Jews were divided because of what Jesus said. [20] Many of them said, "He's possessed by a demon! He's crazy! Why do you listen to him?" [21] Others said, "No one talks like this if he's possessed by a demon. Can a demon give sight to the blind?"

The Jews Reject Jesus

[22] The Festival of the Dedication of the Temple took place in Jerusalem during the winter. [23] Jesus was walking on Solomon's porch in the temple courtyard.

²⁴ The Jews surrounded him. They asked him, "How long will you keep us in suspense? If you are the Messiah, tell us plainly."

²⁵ Jesus answered them, "I've told you, but you don't believe me. The things that I do in my Father's name testify on my behalf. ²⁶ However, you don't believe because you're not my sheep. ²⁷ *My sheep respond to my voice, and I know who they are. They follow me,* ²⁸ *and I give them eternal life. They will never be lost, and no one will tear them away from me.* ²⁹ *My Father, who gave them to me, is greater than everyone else, and no one can tear them away from my Father.* ³⁰ *The Father and I are one."* **(Turn to page 44.)**

³¹ The Jews had again brought some rocks to stone Jesus to death. ³² Jesus replied to them, "I've shown you many good things that come from the Father. For which of these good things do you want to stone me to death?"

³³ The Jews answered Jesus, "We're going to stone you to death, not for any good things you've done, but for dishonoring God. You claim to be God, although you're only a man."

³⁴ Jesus said to them, "Don't your Scriptures say, 'I said, "You are gods"'? ³⁵ The Scriptures cannot be discredited. So if God calls people gods (and they are the people to whom he gave the Scriptures), ³⁶ why do you say that I'm dishonoring God because I said, 'I'm the Son of God'? God set me apart for this holy purpose and has sent me into the world. ³⁷ If I'm not doing the things my Father does, don't believe me. ³⁸ But if I'm doing those things and you refuse to believe me, then at least believe the things that I'm doing. Then you will know and recognize that the Father is in me and that I am in the Father."

³⁹ The Jews tried to arrest Jesus again, but he got away from them. ⁴⁰ He went back across the Jordan River and stayed in the place where John first baptized people.

⁴¹ Many people went to Jesus. They said, "John didn't perform any miracles, but everything John said about this man is true." ⁴² Many people there believed in Jesus.

Jesus Brings Lazarus Back to Life

¹ Lazarus, who lived in Bethany, the village where Mary and her sister Martha lived, was sick. ² (Mary was the woman who poured perfume on the Lord and wiped his feet with her hair. Her brother Lazarus was the one who was sick.)

³ So the sisters sent a messenger to tell Jesus, "Lord, your close friend is sick."

⁴ When Jesus heard the message, he said, "His sickness won't result in death. Instead, this sickness will bring glory to God so that the Son of God will receive glory through it."

⁵ Jesus loved Martha, her sister, and Lazarus. ⁶ Yet, when Jesus heard that Lazarus was sick, he stayed where he was for two more days.

⁷ Then, after the two days, Jesus said to his disciples, "Let's go back to Judea."

⁸ The disciples said to him, "Rabbi, not long ago the Jews wanted to stone you to death. Do you really want to go back there?"

⁹ Jesus answered, "Aren't there twelve hours of daylight? Those who walk during the day don't stumble, because they see the light of this world. ¹⁰ However, those who walk at night stumble because they have no light in themselves."

¹¹ After Jesus said this, he told his disciples, "Our friend Lazarus is sleeping, and I'm going to Bethany to wake him."

¹² His disciples said to him, "Lord, if he's sleeping, he'll get well."

¹³ Jesus meant that Lazarus was dead, but the disciples thought Jesus meant that Lazarus was only sleeping. ¹⁴ Then Jesus told them plainly, "Lazarus has died, ¹⁵ but

I'm glad that I wasn't there so that you can grow in faith. Let's go to Lazarus."

[16] Thomas, who was called Didymus, said to the rest of the disciples, "Let's go so that we, too, can die with Jesus."

[17] When Jesus arrived, he found that Lazarus had been in the tomb for four days. [18] (Bethany was near Jerusalem, not quite two miles away.) [19] Many Jews had come to Martha and Mary to comfort them about their brother.

[20] When Martha heard that Jesus was coming, she went to meet him. Mary stayed at home. [21] Martha told Jesus, "Lord, if you had been here, my brother would not have died. [22] But even now I know that God will give you whatever you ask him."

[23] Jesus told Martha, "Your brother will come back to life."

[24] Martha answered Jesus, "I know that he'll come back to life on the last day, when everyone will come back to life."

[25] Jesus said to her, "I am the one who brings people back to life, and I am life itself. Those who believe in me will live even if they die. [26] Everyone who lives and believes in me will never die. Do you believe that?"

[27] Martha said to him, "Yes, Lord, I believe that you are the Messiah, the Son of God, the one who was expected to come into the world."

[28] After Martha had said this, she went back home and whispered to her sister Mary, "The teacher is here, and he is calling for you."

[29] When Mary heard this, she got up quickly and went to Jesus. [30] (Jesus had not yet come into the village but was still where Martha had met him.) [31] The Jews who were comforting Mary in the house saw her get up quickly and leave. So they followed her. They thought that she was going to the tomb to cry. [32] When Mary arrived where Jesus was and saw him, she knelt at his feet

> **GOD'S LOVE FOR US**
>
> When bad events happen, we might question God's love for us. When Mary's brother Lazarus died, she questioned Jesus. Mary thought that if Jesus had been there, Lazarus would still be alive. Jesus knew that God had a greater plan. There may be times when you can't understand what God is doing. But if you trust his love, you will eventually see God's greater plan. No matter what your difficult situation may be, trust God's love. Although you don't understand what has happened, you can trust God to work out the events in your life. Discover what God's greater plan was for Lazarus in John 11:28-44.

and said, "Lord, if you had been here, my brother would not have died."

[33] When Jesus saw her crying, and the Jews who were crying with her, he was deeply moved and troubled.

[34] So Jesus asked, "Where did you put Lazarus?"

They answered him, "Lord, come and see."

[35] Jesus cried. [36] The Jews said, "See how much Jesus loved him." [37] But some of the Jews asked, "Couldn't this man who gave a blind man sight keep Lazarus from dying?"

[38] Deeply moved again, Jesus went to the tomb. It was a cave with a stone covering the entrance. [39] Jesus said, "Take the stone away."

Martha, the dead man's sister, told Jesus, "Lord, there must already be a stench. He's been dead for four days."

[40] Jesus said to her, "Didn't I tell you that if you believe, you would see God's glory?" [41] So the stone was moved away from the entrance of the tomb.

Jesus looked up and said, "Father, I thank you for hearing me. [42] I've known that you always hear me. However, I've said this so that the crowd standing around me will believe that you sent me." [43] After Jesus had said this, he shouted as loudly as he could, "Lazarus, come out!"

[44] The dead man came out. Strips of cloth were wound around his feet and hands, and his face was wrapped with a handkerchief. Jesus told them, "Free Lazarus, and let him go."

The Jewish Council Plans to Kill Jesus

[45] Many Jews who had visited Mary and had seen what Jesus had done believed in him. [46] But some of them went to the Pharisees and told them what Jesus had done. [47] So the chief priests and the Pharisees called a meeting of the council. They asked, "What are we doing? This man is performing a lot of miracles. [48] If we let him continue what he's doing, everyone will believe in him. Then the Romans will take away our position and our nation."

[49] One of them, Caiaphas, who was chief priest that year, told them, "You people don't know anything. [50] You haven't even considered this: It is better for one man to die for the people than for the whole nation to be destroyed."

[51] Caiaphas didn't say this on his own. As chief priest that year, he prophesied that Jesus would die for the Jewish nation. [52] He prophesied that Jesus wouldn't die merely for this nation, but that Jesus would die to bring God's scattered children together and make them one.

[53] From that day on, the Jewish council planned to kill Jesus. [54] So Jesus no longer walked openly among the Jews. Instead, he left Bethany and went to the countryside near the desert, to a city called Ephraim, where he stayed with his disciples.

[55] The Jewish Passover was near. Many people came from the countryside to Jerusalem to purify themselves before the Passover. [56] As they stood in the temple courtyard, they looked for Jesus and asked each other, "Do you think that he'll avoid coming to the festival?" [57] (The chief priests and the Pharisees had given orders that whoever knew where Jesus was should tell them so that they could arrest him.)

Mary Prepares Jesus' Body for the Tomb

[1] Six days before Passover, Jesus arrived in Bethany. Lazarus, whom Jesus had brought back to life, lived

there. ² Dinner was prepared for Jesus in Bethany. Martha served the dinner, and Lazarus was one of the people eating with Jesus.

³ Mary took a bottle of very expensive perfume made from pure nard and poured it on Jesus' feet. Then she dried his feet with her hair. The fragrance of the perfume filled the house.

⁴ One of his disciples, Judas Iscariot, who was going to betray him, asked, ⁵ "Why wasn't this perfume sold for a high price and the money given to the poor?" ⁶ (Judas didn't say this because he cared about the poor but because he was a thief. He was in charge of the moneybag and carried the contributions.) ⁷ Jesus said to Judas, "Leave her alone! She has done this to prepare me for the day I will be placed in a tomb. ⁸ You will always have the poor with you, but you will not always have me with you."

⁹ A large crowd of Jews found out that Jesus was in Bethany. So they went there not only to see Jesus but also to see Lazarus, whom Jesus had brought back to life. ¹⁰ The chief priests planned to kill Lazarus too. ¹¹ Lazarus was the reason why many people were leaving the Jews and believing in Jesus.

The King Comes to Jerusalem

¹² On the next day the large crowd that had come to the Passover festival heard that Jesus was coming to Jerusalem. ¹³ So they took palm branches and went to meet him. They were shouting,

> "Hosanna!
> Blessed is the one who comes in the name of the Lord, the king of Israel!"

¹⁴ Jesus obtained a donkey and sat on it, as Scripture says:
¹⁵ "Don't be afraid, people of Zion!
Your king is coming.
He is riding on a donkey's colt."

[16] At first Jesus' disciples didn't know what these prophecies meant. However, when Jesus was glorified, the disciples remembered that these prophecies had been written about him. The disciples remembered that they had taken part in fulfilling the prophecies.

[17] The people who had been with Jesus when he called Lazarus from the tomb and brought him back to life reported what they had seen. [18] Because the crowd heard that Jesus had performed this miracle, they came to meet him.

[19] The Pharisees said to each other, "This is getting us nowhere. Look! The whole world is following him!"

Some Greeks Ask to See Jesus

[20] Some Greeks were among those who came to worship during the Passover festival. [21] They went to Philip (who was from Bethsaida in Galilee) and told him, "Sir, we would like to meet Jesus." [22] Philip told Andrew, and they told Jesus.

[23] Jesus replied to them, "The time has come for the Son of Man to be glorified. [24] I can guarantee this truth: A single grain of wheat doesn't produce anything unless it is planted in the ground and dies. If it dies, it will produce a lot of grain. [25] Those who love their lives will destroy them, and those who hate their lives in this world will guard them for everlasting life. [26] Those who serve me must follow me. My servants will be with me wherever I will be. If people serve me, the Father will honor them.

[27] "I am too deeply troubled now to know how to express my feelings. Should I say, 'Father, save me from this time [of suffering]'? No! I came for this time of suffering. [28] Father, give glory to your name."

A voice from heaven said, "I have given it glory, and I will give it glory again."

²⁹ The crowd standing there heard the voice and said that it had thundered. Others in the crowd said that an angel had talked to him. ³⁰ Jesus replied, "That voice wasn't for my benefit but for yours.

³¹ "This world is being judged now. The ruler of this world will be thrown out now. ³² When I have been lifted up from the earth, I will draw all people toward me." ³³ By saying this, he indicated how he was going to die.

³⁴ The crowd responded to him, "We have heard from the Scriptures that the Messiah will remain here forever. So how can you say, 'The Son of Man must be lifted up from the earth'? Who is this 'Son of Man'?"

³⁵ Jesus answered the crowd, "The light will still be with you for a little while. Walk while you have light so that darkness won't defeat you. Those who walk in the dark don't know where they're going. ³⁶ While you have the light, believe in the light so that you will become people whose lives show the light."

After Jesus had said this, he was concealed as he left. ³⁷ Although they had seen Jesus perform so many miracles, they wouldn't believe in him. ³⁸ In this way the words of the prophet Isaiah came true:

"Lord, who has believed our message?
To whom has the Lord's power been revealed?"

³⁹ So the people couldn't believe because, as Isaiah also said,

⁴⁰"God blinded them
and made them close-minded
so that their eyes don't see
and their minds don't understand.
And they never turn to me for healing!"

⁴¹ Isaiah said this because he had seen Jesus' glory and had spoken about him.

⁴² Many rulers believed in Jesus. However, they wouldn't admit it publicly because the Pharisees would have thrown them out of the synagogue. ⁴³ They were more concerned

about what people thought of them than about what God thought of them.

⁴⁴ Then Jesus said loudly, "Whoever believes in me believes not only in me but also in the one who sent me. ⁴⁵ Whoever sees me sees the one who sent me. ⁴⁶ I am the light that has come into the world so that everyone who believes in me will not live in the dark. ⁴⁷ If anyone hears my words and doesn't follow them, I don't condemn them. I didn't come to condemn the world but to save the world. ⁴⁸ Those who reject me by not accepting what I say have a judge appointed for them. The words that I have spoken will judge them on the last day. ⁴⁹ I have not spoken on my own. Instead, the Father who sent me told me what I should say and how I should say it. ⁵⁰ I know that what he commands is eternal life. Whatever I say is what the Father told me to say."

Jesus Washes the Disciples' Feet

¹ Before the Passover festival, Jesus knew that the time had come for him to leave this world and go back to the Father. Jesus loved his own who were in the world, and he loved them to the end.

² While supper was taking place, the devil had already put the idea of betraying Jesus into the mind of Judas, son of Simon Iscariot.

³ The Father had put everything in Jesus' control. Jesus knew that. He also knew that he had come from God and was going back to God. ⁴ So he got up from the table, removed his outer clothes, took a towel, and tied it around his waist. ⁵ Then he poured water into a basin and began to wash the disciples' feet and dry them with the towel that he had tied around his waist.

⁶ When Jesus came to Simon Peter, Peter asked him, "Lord, are you going to wash my feet?"

⁷ Jesus answered Peter, "You don't know now what I'm doing. You will understand later."

⁸ Peter told Jesus, "You will never wash my feet."

Jesus replied to Peter, "If I don't wash you, you don't belong to me."

⁹ Simon Peter said to Jesus, "Lord, don't wash only my feet. Wash my hands and my head too!"

¹⁰ Jesus told Peter, "People who have washed are completely clean. They need to have only their feet washed. All of you, except for one, are clean." ¹¹ (Jesus knew who was going to betray him. That's why he said, "All of you, except for one, are clean.")

> **CARING FOR OTHERS**
>
> Did you see the irony in John 13:3-5? Jesus, King of the universe, cleaned between his servants' dirty toes. The example for us is clear. None of us is better than another, and no one should expect to be served. Rather than expect someone to serve you, look for ways to serve someone else. Imitate Jesus' example.

¹² After Jesus had washed their feet and put on his outer clothes, he took his place at the table again. Then he asked his disciples, "Do you understand what I've done for you? ¹³ You call me teacher and Lord, and you're right because that's what I am. ¹⁴ So if I, your Lord and teacher, have washed your feet, you must wash each other's feet. ¹⁵ I've given you an example that you should follow. ¹⁶ I can guarantee this truth: Slaves are not superior to their owners, and messengers are not superior to the people who send them. ¹⁷ If you understand all of this, you are blessed whenever you follow my example.

¹⁸ "I'm not talking about all of you. I know the people I've chosen [to be apostles]. However, I've made my choice so that Scripture will come true. It says, 'The one who eats my bread has turned against me.' ¹⁹ I'm telling you now before it happens. Then, when it happens, you will believe that I am the one.

²⁰ "I can guarantee this truth: Whoever accepts me accepts the one who sent me."

Jesus Knows Who Will Betray Him

²¹ After saying this, Jesus was deeply troubled. He declared, "I can guarantee this truth: One of you is going to betray me!"

²² The disciples began looking at each other and wondering which one of them Jesus meant.

²³ One disciple, the one whom Jesus loved, was near him at the table. ²⁴ Simon Peter motioned to that disciple and said, "Ask Jesus whom he's talking about!"

²⁵ Leaning close to Jesus, that disciple asked, "Lord, who is it?"

²⁶ Jesus answered, "He's the one to whom I will give this piece of bread after I've dipped it in the sauce." So Jesus dipped the bread and gave it to Judas, son of Simon Iscariot.

²⁷ Then, after Judas took the piece of bread, Satan entered him. So Jesus told him, "Hurry! Do what you have to do." ²⁸ No one at the table knew why Jesus said this to him. ²⁹ Judas had the moneybag. So some thought that Jesus was telling him to buy what they needed for the festival or to give something to the poor.

³⁰ Judas took the piece of bread and immediately went outside. It was night.

³¹ When Judas was gone, Jesus said, "The Son of Man is now glorified, and because of him God is glorified. ³² If God is glorified because of the Son of Man, God will glorify the Son of Man because of himself, and he will glorify the Son of Man at once."

Jesus Predicts Peter's Denial

³³ Jesus said, "Dear children, I will still be with you for a little while. I'm telling you what I told the Jews. You will look for me, but you can't go where I'm going.

³⁴ "I'm giving you a new commandment: Love each other in the same way that I have loved you. ³⁵ Everyone will know that you are my disciples because of your love for each other."

> **LOVING GOD AND OTHERS**
>
> What do your actions say to others about your faith? During his last supper with his disciples, Jesus urged them to love each other. When we love each other, we demonstrate that we are also disciples of Jesus, the Savior. What do your actions tell others? Would someone know you are a disciple of Jesus by watching what you do? Find Jesus' command to love one another in John 13:34-35.

[36] Simon Peter asked him, "Lord, where are you going?"

Jesus answered him, "You can't follow me now to the place where I'm going. However, you will follow me later."

[37] Peter said to Jesus, "Lord, why can't I follow you now? I'll give my life for you."

[38] Jesus replied, "Will you give your life for me? I can guarantee this truth: No rooster will crow until you say three times that you don't know me.

Jesus Promises to Send the Holy Spirit

[1] "Don't be troubled. Believe in God, and believe in me. [2] My Father's house has many rooms. If that were not true, would I have told you that I'm going to prepare a place for you? [3] If I go to prepare a place for you, I will come again. Then I will bring you into my presence so that you will be where I am. [4] You know the way to the place where I am going."

[5] Thomas said to him, "Lord, we don't know where you're going. So how can we know the way?"

[6] Jesus answered him, "**I am the way, the truth, and the life. No one goes to the Father except through me. [7] If you have known me, you will also know my Father. From now on you know him ⌊through me⌋ and have seen him ⌊in me⌋.**" (Turn to page 45.)

[8] Philip said to Jesus, "Lord, show us the Father, and that will satisfy us."

[9] Jesus replied, "I have been with all of you for a long time. Don't you know me yet, Philip? The person who has

seen me has seen the Father. So how can you say, 'Show us the Father'? ¹⁰ Don't you believe that I am in the Father and the Father is in me? What I'm telling you doesn't come from me. The Father, who lives in me, does what he wants. ¹¹ Believe me when I say that I am in the Father and that the Father is in me. Otherwise, believe me because of the things I do.

¹² "I can guarantee this truth: Those who believe in me will do the things that I am doing. They will do even greater things because I am going to the Father. ¹³ I will do anything you ask [the Father] in my name so that the Father will be given glory because of the Son. ¹⁴ If you ask me to do something, I will do it.

¹⁵ **"If you love me, you will obey my commandments. ¹⁶ I will ask the Father, and he will give you another helper who will be with you forever. ¹⁷ That helper is the Spirit of Truth. The world cannot accept him, because it doesn't see or know him. You know him, because he lives with you and will be in you.** (Turn to page 46.)

¹⁸ "I will not leave you all alone. I will come back to you. ¹⁹ In a little while the world will no longer see me, but you will see me. You will live because I live. ²⁰ On that day you will know that I am in my Father and that you are in me and that I am in you. ²¹ Whoever knows and obeys my commandments is the person who loves me. Those who love me will have my Father's love, and I, too, will love them and show myself to them."

²² Judas (not Iscariot) asked Jesus, "Lord, what has happened that you are going to reveal yourself to us and not to the world?"

²³ Jesus answered him, "Those who love me will do what I say. My Father will love them, and we will go to them and make our home with them. ²⁴ A person who doesn't love me doesn't do what I say. I don't make up

what you hear me say. What I say comes from the Father who sent me.

[25] "I have told you this while I'm still with you. [26] However, the helper, the Holy Spirit, whom the Father will send in my name, will teach you everything. He will remind you of everything that I have ever told you.

[27] *"I'm leaving you peace. I'm giving you my peace. I don't give you the kind of peace that the world gives. So don't be troubled or cowardly. (Turn to page 51.)* [28] You heard me tell you, 'I'm going away, but I'm coming back to you.' If you loved me, you would be glad that I'm going to the Father, because the Father is greater than I am.

[29] "I'm telling you this now before it happens. When it does happen, you will believe. [30] The ruler of this world has no power over me. But he's coming, so I won't talk with you much longer. [31] However, I want the world to know that I love the Father and that I am doing exactly what the Father has commanded me to do. Get up! We have to leave."

HOLY SPIRIT

Do you want help? Would you like comfort? Are you looking for peace? Do you need assurance of love or protection? Would you like to remember Jesus' teachings? The Holy Spirit provides all these things and more to those who are Christians. Jesus told his disciples about the Holy Spirit who would come to be with each of them—and all his followers—forever. Read more about what Jesus told them in John 14:25-28.

Jesus, the True Vine

[1] ⌊Then Jesus said,⌋ "I am the true vine, and my Father takes care of the vineyard. [2] He removes every one of my branches that doesn't produce fruit. He also prunes every branch that does produce fruit to make it produce more fruit.

[3] "You are already clean because of what I have told you. [4] Live in me, and I will live in you. A branch cannot produce

any fruit by itself. It has to stay attached to the vine. In the same way, you cannot produce fruit unless you live in me.

⁵ "I am the vine. You are the branches. Those who live in me while I live in them will produce a lot of fruit. But you can't produce anything without me. ⁶ Whoever doesn't live in me is thrown away like a branch and dries up. Branches like this are gathered, thrown into a fire, and burned. ⁷ If you live in me and what I say lives in you, then ask for anything you want, and it will be yours. ⁸ You give glory to my Father when you produce a lot of fruit and therefore show that you are my disciples.

⁹ "I have loved you the same way the Father has loved me. So live in my love. ¹⁰ If you obey my commandments, you will live in my love. I have obeyed my Father's commandments, and in that way I live in his love. ¹¹ I have told you this so that you will be as joyful as I am, and your joy will be complete. ¹² Love each other as I have loved you. This is what I'm commanding you to do. ¹³ The greatest love you can show is to give your life for your friends. ¹⁴ You are my friends if you obey my commandments. ¹⁵ I don't call you servants anymore, because a servant doesn't know what his master is doing. But I've called you friends because I've made known to you everything that I've heard from my Father. ¹⁶ You didn't choose me, but I chose you. I have appointed you to go, to produce fruit that will last, and to ask the Father in my name to give you whatever you ask for. ¹⁷ Love each other. This is what I'm commanding you to do.

¹⁸ "If the world hates you, realize that it hated me before it hated you. ¹⁹ If you had anything in common with the world, the world would love you as one of its own. But you don't have anything in common with the world. I chose you from the world, and that's why the world hates you. ²⁰ Remember what I told you: 'A servant

isn't greater than his master.' If they persecuted me, they will also persecute you. If they did what I said, they will also do what you say. ²¹ Indeed, they will do all this to you because you are committed to me, since they don't know the one who sent me. ²² If I hadn't come and spoken to them, they wouldn't have any sin. But now they have no excuse for their sin. ²³ The person who hates me also hates my Father. ²⁴ If I hadn't done among them what no one else has done, they wouldn't have any sin. But now they have seen and hated both me and my Father. ²⁵ In this way what is written in their Scriptures has come true: 'They hate me for no reason.'

²⁶ "The helper whom I will send to you from the Father will come. This helper, the Spirit of Truth who comes from the Father, will declare the truth about me. ²⁷ You will declare the truth, too, because you have been with me from the beginning."

WITNESSING

When you tell others about how you came to know Christ, you give your friends one of the strongest arguments for becoming a Christian. You alone are an expert witness on the difference Jesus makes. Your friends may question the Bible, but they cannot doubt what happened to you. They may argue about the existence of God, but they cannot explain away your own testimony of his work in your life. That is why Jesus commands us to testify about him. Read about it in John 15:26-27.

Sadness Will Turn to Joy

¹ ⌊Jesus continued,⌋ "I have said these things to you so that you won't lose your faith. ² You will be thrown out of synagogues. Certainly, the time is coming when people who murder you will think that they are serving God. ³ They will do these things to you because they haven't known the Father or me. ⁴ But I've told you this so that when it happens you'll remember what I've told you. I didn't tell you this at first, because I was with you.

⁵ "Now I'm going to the one who sent me. Yet, none of you asks me where I'm going. ⁶ But because I've told you

this, you're filled with sadness. [7] However, I am telling you the truth: It's good for you that I'm going away. If I don't go away, the helper won't come to you. But if I go, I will send him to you. [8] He will come to convict the world of sin, to show the world what has God's approval, and to convince the world that God judges it. [9] He will convict the world of sin, because people don't believe in me. [10] He will show the world what has God's approval, because I'm going to the Father and you won't see me anymore. [11] He will convince the world that God judges it, because the ruler of this world has been judged.

[12] "I have a lot more to tell you, but that would be too much for you now. [13] When the Spirit of Truth comes, he will guide you into the full truth. He won't speak on his own. He will speak what he hears and will tell you about things to come. [14] He will give me glory, because he will tell you what I say. [15] Everything the Father says is also what I say. That is why I said, 'He will take what I say and tell it to you.'

[16] "In a little while you won't see me anymore. Then in a little while you will see me again."

[17] Some of his disciples said to each other, "What does he mean? He tells us that in a little while we won't see him. Then he tells us that in a little while we will see him again and that he's going to the Father." [18] So they were asking each other, "What does he mean when he says, 'In a little while'? We don't understand what he's talking about."

FEELINGS

As your relationship with Christ matures, you will begin to notice changes in your feelings and emotions. You will find that your emotions respond more and more to what affects the heart of God. You will be disturbed by sin in the world and in your own life. Your heart will ache over a friend's disinterest in Christ. But you will also experience joy that will last forever because you know God. Read more about the joys and sorrows that Jesus said were in store for his disciples in John 16:6-15.

[19] Jesus knew they wanted to ask him something. So he said to them, "Are you trying to figure out among yourselves what I meant when I said, 'In a little while you won't see me, and in a little while you will see me again'? [20] I can guarantee this truth: You will cry because you are sad, but the world will be happy. You will feel pain, but your pain will turn to happiness. [21] A woman has pain when her time to give birth comes. But after the child is born, she doesn't remember the pain anymore because she's happy that a child has been brought into the world.

[22] "Now you're in a painful situation. But I will see you again. Then you will be happy, and no one will take that happiness away from you. [23] When that day comes, you won't ask me any more questions. I can guarantee this truth: If you ask the Father for anything in my name, he will give it to you. [24] So far you haven't asked for anything in my name. Ask and you will receive so that you can be completely happy.

[25] "I have used examples to illustrate these things. The time is coming when I won't use examples to speak to you. Rather, I will speak to you about the Father in plain words. [26] When that day comes, you will ask for what you want in my name. I'm telling you that I won't have to ask the Father for you. [27] The Father loves you because you have loved me and have believed that I came from God. [28] I left the Father and came into the world. Again, [as I've said,] I'm going to leave the world and go back to the Father."

[29] His disciples said, "Now you're talking in plain words and not using examples. [30] Now we know that you know everything. You don't need to wait for questions to be asked. Because of this, we believe that you have come from God."

[31] Jesus replied to them, "Now you believe. [32] The time is coming, and is already here, when all of you will be scattered. Each of you will go your own way and leave me all alone. Yet, I'm not all alone, because the Father is with

me. ³³ *I've told you this so that my peace will be with you. In the world you'll have trouble. But cheer up! I have overcome the world." (Turn to page 62.)*

Jesus Prays for Himself, His Disciples, and His Church

¹ After saying this, Jesus looked up to heaven and said, "Father, the time is here. Give your Son glory so that your Son can give you glory. ² After all, you've given him authority over all humanity so that he can give eternal life to all those you gave to him. ³ This is eternal life: to know you, the only true God, and Jesus Christ, whom you sent. ⁴ On earth I have given you glory by finishing the work you gave me to do. ⁵ Now, Father, give me glory in your presence with the glory I had with you before the world existed.

> **PEACE**
>
> Two thousand years ago, Jesus gave his followers something that can be ours today, peace in the middle of craziness. Jesus knows how difficult troubles can be, but he also knows that he is greater than any problem. Read the truth about Jesus in John 16:33.

⁶ "I made your name known to the people you gave me. They are from this world. They belonged to you, and you gave them to me. They did what you told them. ⁷ Now they know that everything you gave me comes from you, ⁸ because I gave them the message that you gave me. They have accepted this message, and they know for sure that I came from you. They have believed that you sent me.

⁹ "I pray for them. I'm not praying for the world but for those you gave me, because they are yours. ¹⁰ Everything I have is yours, and everything you have is mine. I have been given glory by the people you have given me. ¹¹ I won't be in the world much longer, but they are in the world, and I'm coming back to you. Holy Father, keep them safe by the power of your name, the

> ## POPULARITY
>
> Like a square peg trying to fit into a round hole, you attempt the impossible when you try to fit in with the rest of the world. In John 17:14-17, Jesus prayed for Christians to realize they will never belong in a group of people who live according to the world's standards. And yet sometimes you may still struggle to feel totally accepted and understood by friends and family members who are not Christians. The world will never fully accept you because of the difference Christ has made in you. Rather than feel depressed that you don't fit in, be glad that you belong instead to Christ.

name that you gave me, so that their unity may be like ours. ¹² While I was with them, I kept them safe by the power of your name, the name that you gave me. I watched over them, and none of them, except one person, became lost. So Scripture came true.

¹³ "But now, ⌊Father,⌋ I'm coming back to you. I say these things while I'm still in the world so that they will have the same joy that I have. ¹⁴ I have given them your message. But the world has hated them because they don't belong to the world any more than I belong to the world. ¹⁵ I'm not asking you to take them out of the world but to protect them from the evil one. ¹⁶ They don't belong to the world any more than I belong to the world.

¹⁷ "Use the truth to make them holy. Your words are truth. ¹⁸ I have sent them into the world the same way you sent me into the world. ¹⁹ I'm dedicating myself to this holy work I'm doing for them so that they, too, will use the truth to be holy.

²⁰ "I'm not praying only for them. I'm also praying for those who will believe in me through their message. ²¹ I pray that all of these people continue to have unity in the way that you, Father, are in me and I am in you. I pray that they may be united with us so that the world will believe that you have sent me. ²² I have given them the glory that you gave me. I did this so that they are united in the same

way we are. ²³ I am in them, and you are in me. So they are completely united. In this way the world knows that you have sent me and that you have loved them in the same way you have loved me.

²⁴ "Father, I want those you have given to me to be with me, to be where I am. I want them to see my glory, which you gave me because you loved me before the world was made. ²⁵ Righteous Father, the world didn't know you. Yet, I knew you, and these ⌊disciples⌋ have known that you sent me. ²⁶ I have made your name known to them, and I will make it known so that the love you have for me will be in them and I will be in them."

Jesus Is Arrested

¹ After Jesus finished his prayer, he went with his disciples to the other side of the Kidron Valley. They entered the garden that was there.

² Judas, who betrayed him, knew the place because Jesus and his disciples often gathered there. ³ So Judas took a troop of soldiers and the guards from the chief priests and Pharisees and went to the garden. They were carrying lanterns, torches, and weapons.

⁴ Jesus knew everything that was going to happen to him. So he went to meet them and asked, "Who are you looking for?"

⁵ They answered him, "Jesus from Nazareth."

Jesus told them, "I am he."

Judas, who betrayed him, was standing with the crowd. ⁶ When Jesus told them, "I am he," the crowd backed away and fell to the ground.

⁷ Jesus asked them again, "Who are you looking for?"

They said, "Jesus from Nazareth."

⁸ Jesus replied, "I told you that I am he. So if you are looking for me, let these other men go." ⁹ In this way what Jesus had said came true: "I lost none of those you gave me."

¹⁰ Simon Peter had a sword. He drew it, attacked the chief priest's servant, and cut off the servant's right ear. (The servant's name was Malchus.)

¹¹ Jesus told Peter, "Put your sword away. Shouldn't I drink the cup ⌊of suffering⌋ that my Father has given me?"

¹² Then the army officer and the Jewish guards arrested Jesus. They tied Jesus up ¹³ and took him first to Annas, the father-in-law of Caiaphas. Caiaphas, the chief priest that year, ¹⁴ was the person who had advised the Jews that it was better to have one man die for the people.

Peter Denies Jesus

¹⁵ Simon Peter and another disciple followed Jesus. The other disciple was well-known to the chief priest. So that disciple went with Jesus into the chief priest's courtyard. ¹⁶ Peter, however, was standing outside the gate. The other disciple talked to the woman who was the gatekeeper and brought Peter into the courtyard.

¹⁷ The gatekeeper asked Peter, "Aren't you one of this man's disciples too?"

Peter answered, "No, I'm not!"

¹⁸ The servants and the guards were standing around a fire they had built and were warming themselves because it was cold. Peter was standing there, too, and warming himself with the others.

The Chief Priest Questions Jesus

¹⁹ The chief priest questioned Jesus about his disciples and his teachings.

²⁰ Jesus answered him, "I have spoken publicly for everyone to hear. I have always taught in synagogues or in the temple courtyard, where all the Jews gather. I haven't said anything in secret. ²¹ Why do you question me? Question those who heard what I said to them. They know what I've said."

²² When Jesus said this, one of the guards standing near Jesus slapped his face and said, "Is that how you answer the chief priest?"

²³ Jesus replied to him, "If I've said anything wrong, tell me what it was. But if I've told the truth, why do you hit me?"

²⁴ Annas sent Jesus to Caiaphas, the chief priest. Jesus was still tied up.

Peter Denies Jesus Again

²⁵ Simon Peter continued to stand and warm himself by the fire. Some men asked him, "Aren't you, too, one of his disciples?"

Peter denied it by saying, "No, I'm not!"

²⁶ One of the chief priest's servants, a relative of the man whose ear Peter had cut off, asked him, "Didn't I see you with Jesus in the garden?"

²⁷ Peter again denied it, and just then a rooster crowed.

Pilate Questions Jesus

²⁸ Early in the morning, Jesus was taken from Caiaphas' house to the governor's palace.

The Jews wouldn't go into the palace. They didn't want to become unclean, since they wanted to eat the Passover. ²⁹ So Pilate came out to them and asked, "What accusation are you making against this man?"

³⁰ The Jews answered Pilate, "If he weren't a criminal, we wouldn't have handed him over to you."

³¹ Pilate told the Jews, "Take him, and try him by your law."

The Jews answered him, "We're not allowed to execute anyone." ³² In this way what Jesus had predicted about how he would die came true.

³³ Pilate went back into the palace, called for Jesus, and asked him, "Are you the king of the Jews?"

[34] Jesus replied, "Did you think of that yourself, or did others tell you about me?"

[35] Pilate answered, "Am I a Jew? Your own people and the chief priests handed you over to me. What have you done?"

[36] Jesus answered, "My kingdom doesn't belong to this world. If my kingdom belonged to this world, my followers would fight to keep me from being handed over to the Jews. My kingdom doesn't have its origin on earth."

[37] Pilate asked him, "So you are a king?"

Jesus replied, "You're correct in saying that I'm a king. I have been born and have come into the world for this reason: to testify to the truth. Everyone who belongs to the truth listens to me."

[38] Pilate said to him, "What is truth?"

After Pilate said this, he went out to the Jews again and told them, "I don't find this man guilty of anything. [39] You have a custom that I should free one person for you at Passover. Would you like me to free the king of the Jews for you?"

[40] The Jews shouted again, "Don't free this man! Free Barabbas!" (Barabbas was a political revolutionary.)

The Soldiers Make Fun of Jesus

[1] Then Pilate had Jesus taken away and whipped. [2] The soldiers twisted some thorny branches into a crown, placed it on his head, and put a purple cape on him. [3] They went up to him, said, "Long live the king of the Jews!" and slapped his face.

The People Want Jesus Crucified

[4] Pilate went outside again and told the Jews, "I'm bringing him out to you to let you know that I don't find this man guilty of anything." [5] Jesus went outside. He was wearing the crown of thorns and the purple cape. Pilate said to the Jews, "Look, here's the man!"

⁶ When the chief priests and the guards saw Jesus, they shouted, "Crucify him! Crucify him!"

Pilate told them, "You take him and crucify him. I don't find this man guilty of anything."

⁷ The Jews answered Pilate, "We have a law, and by that law he must die because he claimed to be the Son of God."

⁸ When Pilate heard them say that, he became more afraid than ever. ⁹ He went into the palace again and asked Jesus, "Where are you from?" But Jesus didn't answer him.

¹⁰ So Pilate said to Jesus, "Aren't you going to answer me? Don't you know that I have the authority to free you or to crucify you?"

¹¹ Jesus answered Pilate, "You wouldn't have any authority over me if it hadn't been given to you from above. That's why the man who handed me over to you is guilty of a greater sin."

¹² When Pilate heard what Jesus said, he wanted to free him. But the Jews shouted, "If you free this man, you're not a friend of the emperor. Anyone who claims to be a king is defying the emperor."

¹³ When Pilate heard what they said, he took Jesus outside and sat on the judge's seat in a place called Stone Pavement. (In Hebrew it is called *Gabbatha*.) ¹⁴ The time was about six o'clock in the morning on the Friday of the Passover festival.

Pilate said to the Jews, "Look, here's your king!"

¹⁵ Then the Jews shouted, "Kill him! Kill him! Crucify him!"

Pilate asked them, "Should I crucify your king?"

The chief priests responded, "The emperor is the only king we have!"

¹⁶ Then Pilate handed Jesus over to them to be crucified.

The Crucifixion

So the soldiers took Jesus. [17] He carried his own cross and went out ⌊of the city⌋ to a location called The Skull. (In Hebrew this place is called *Golgotha*.) [18] The soldiers crucified Jesus and two other men there. Jesus was in the middle.

[19] Pilate wrote a notice and put it on the cross. The notice read, "Jesus from Nazareth, the king of the Jews." [20] Many Jews read this notice, because the place where Jesus was crucified was near the city. The notice was written in Hebrew, Latin, and Greek.

[21] The chief priests of the Jewish people told Pilate, "Don't write, 'The king of the Jews!' Instead, write, 'He said that he is the king of the Jews.'"

[22] Pilate replied, "I have written what I've written."

[23] When the soldiers had crucified Jesus, they took his clothes and divided them four ways so that each soldier could have a share. His robe was left over. It didn't have a seam because it had been woven in one piece from top to bottom. [24] The soldiers said to each other, "Let's not rip it apart. Let's throw dice to see who will get it." In this way the Scripture came true: "They divided my clothes among themselves. They threw dice for my clothing." So that's what the soldiers did.

[25] Jesus' mother, her sister, Mary (the wife of Clopas), and Mary from Magdala were standing beside Jesus' cross. [26] Jesus saw his mother and the disciple whom he loved standing there. He said to his mother, "Look, here's your

---

FAMILY

Can you imagine what Mary felt standing at the foot of her son's cross? Seeing Jesus in pain, agony, and humiliation must have devastated her. While on the cross, Jesus asked John to take care of his mother. Jesus knew that his mother would need special care and attention in the days to come. How do you feel when you see family members in pain? What can you do to comfort and ease their pain? Read about Jesus' example in John 19:25-27.

son!"²⁷ Then he said to the disciple, "Look, here's your mother!"

From that time on she lived with that disciple in his home.

Jesus Dies on the Cross

²⁸ After this, when Jesus knew that everything had now been finished, he said, "I'm thirsty." He said this so that Scripture could finally be concluded.

²⁹ A jar filled with vinegar was there. So the soldiers put a sponge soaked in the vinegar on a hyssop stick and held it to his mouth.

³⁰ After Jesus had taken the vinegar, he said, "It is finished!"

Then he bowed his head and died.

³¹ Since it was Friday and the next day was an especially important day of worship, the Jews didn't want the bodies to stay on the crosses. So they asked Pilate to have the men's legs broken and their bodies removed. ³² The soldiers broke the legs of the first man and then of the other man who had been crucified with Jesus.

³³ When the soldiers came to Jesus and saw that he was already dead, they didn't break his legs. ³⁴ However, one of the soldiers stabbed Jesus' side with his spear, and blood and water immediately came out. ³⁵ The one who saw this is an eyewitness. What he says is true, and he knows that he is telling the truth so that you, too, will believe.

³⁶ This happened so that the Scripture would come true: "None of his bones will be broken." ³⁷ Another Scripture passage says, "They will look at the person whom they have stabbed."

Jesus Is Buried

³⁸ Later Joseph from the city of Arimathea asked Pilate to let him remove Jesus' body. (Joseph was a disciple of

Jesus but secretly because he was afraid of the Jews). Pilate gave him permission to remove Jesus' body. So Joseph removed it. [39] Nicodemus, the one who had first come to Jesus at night, went with Joseph and brought 75 pounds of a myrrh and aloe mixture.

[40] These two men took the body of Jesus and bound it with strips of linen. They laced the strips with spices. This was the Jewish custom for burial.

[41] A garden was located in the place where Jesus was crucified. In that garden was a new tomb in which no one had yet been placed. [42] Joseph and Nicodemus put Jesus in that tomb, since that day was the Jewish day of preparation and since the tomb was nearby.

Jesus Comes Back to Life

[1] Early on Sunday morning, while it was still dark, Mary from Magdala went to the tomb. She saw that the stone had been removed from the tomb's entrance. [2] So she ran to Simon Peter and the other disciple, whom Jesus loved. She told them, "They have removed the Lord from the tomb, and we don't know where they've put him."

[3] So Peter and the other disciple headed for the tomb. [4] The two were running side by side, but the other disciple ran faster than Peter and came to the tomb first. [5] He bent over and looked inside the tomb. He saw the strips of linen lying there but didn't go inside.

[6] Simon Peter arrived after him and went into the tomb. He saw the strips of linen lying there. [7] He also saw the cloth that had been on Jesus' head. It wasn't lying with the strips of linen but was rolled up separately. [8] Then the other disciple, who arrived at the tomb first, went inside. He saw and believed. [9] They didn't know yet what Scripture meant when it said that Jesus had to come back to life. [10] So the disciples went back home.

Jesus Appears to Mary From Magdala

[11] Mary, however, stood there and cried as she looked at the tomb. As she cried, she bent over and looked inside. [12] She saw two angels in white clothes. They were sitting where the body of Jesus had been lying. One angel was where Jesus' head had been, and the other was where his feet had been. [13] The angels asked her why she was crying.

Mary told them, "They have removed my Lord, and I don't know where they've put him."

[14] After she said this, she turned around and saw Jesus standing there. However, she didn't know that it was Jesus. [15] Jesus asked her, "Why are you crying? Who are you looking for?"

Mary thought it was the gardener speaking to her. So she said to him, "Sir, if you carried him away, tell me where you have put him, and I'll remove him."

[16] Jesus said to her, "Mary!"

Mary turned around and said to him in Hebrew, "Rabboni!" (This word means "teacher.")

[17] Jesus told her, "Don't hold on to me. I have not yet gone to the Father. But go to my brothers and sisters and tell them, 'I am going to my Father and your Father, to my God and your God.'"

[18] Mary from Magdala went to the disciples and told them, "I have seen the Lord." She also told them what he had said to her.

Jesus Appears to the Disciples

[19] That Sunday evening, the disciples were together behind locked doors because they were afraid of the Jews. Jesus stood among them and said to them, "Peace be with you!" [20] When he said this, he showed them his hands and his side. The disciples were glad to see the Lord.

[21] Jesus said to them again, "Peace be with you! As the Father has sent me, so I am sending you." [22] After he had

said this, he breathed on the disciples and said, "Receive the Holy Spirit. [23] Whenever you forgive sins, they are forgiven. Whenever you don't forgive them, they are not forgiven."

Jesus Appears to Thomas

[24] Thomas, one of the twelve apostles, who was called Didymus, wasn't with them when Jesus came. [25] The other disciples told him, "We've seen the Lord."

Thomas told them, "I refuse to believe this unless I see the nail marks in his hands, put my fingers into them, and put my hand into his side."

[26] A week later Jesus' disciples were again in the house, and Thomas was with them. Even though the doors were locked, Jesus stood among them and said, "Peace be with you!" [27] Then Jesus said to Thomas, "Put your finger here, and look at my hands. Take your hand, and put it into my side. Stop doubting, and believe."

[28] Thomas responded to Jesus, "My Lord and my God!"

DOUBT

Thomas, the apostle who doubted, wasn't punished for his reluctance to accept the fact that Jesus came back to life. (Read about it in John 20:24-29.) Instead, Jesus gently allowed him to see the truth for himself. But what an exciting promise Jesus extended to those of us who weren't privileged to walk and talk with him. We will be especially rewarded for believing without seeing. That's a great reminder when doubts arise!

[29] **Jesus said to Thomas, "You believe because you've seen me. Blessed are those who haven't seen me but believe."**

[30] Jesus performed many other miracles that his disciples saw. Those miracles are not written in this book. [31] *But these miracles have been written so that you will believe that Jesus is the Messiah, the Son of God, and so that you will have life by believing in him.*

Jesus Appears to His Disciples Again

¹ Later, by the Sea of Tiberias, Jesus showed himself again to the disciples. This is what happened. ² Simon Peter, Thomas (called Didymus), Nathanael from Cana in Galilee, Zebedee's sons, and two other disciples of Jesus were together. ³ Simon Peter said to the others, "I'm going fishing."

They told him, "We're going with you."

They went out in a boat but didn't catch a thing that night. ⁴ As the sun was rising, Jesus stood on the shore. The disciples didn't realize that it was Jesus.

⁵ Jesus asked them, "Friends, haven't you caught any fish?"

They answered him, "No, we haven't."

⁶ He told them, "Throw the net out on the right side of the boat, and you'll catch some." So they threw the net out and were unable to pull it in because so many fish were in it.

⁷ The disciple whom Jesus loved said to Peter, "It's the Lord." When Simon Peter heard that it was the Lord, he put back on the clothes that he had taken off and jumped into the sea. ⁸ The other disciples came with the boat and dragged the net full of fish. They weren't far from the shore, only about 100 yards.

⁹ When they went ashore, they saw a fire with a fish lying on the coals, and they saw a loaf of bread.

¹⁰ Jesus told them, "Bring some of the fish you've just caught." ¹¹ Simon Peter got into the boat and pulled the net ashore. Though the net was filled with 153 large fish, it was not torn.

¹² Jesus told them, "Come, have breakfast." None of the disciples dared to ask him who he was. They knew he was the Lord. ¹³ Jesus took the bread, gave it to them, and did the same with the fish.

[14] This was the third time that Jesus showed himself to the disciples after he had come back to life.

Jesus Speaks With Peter

[15] After they had eaten breakfast, Jesus asked Simon Peter, "Simon, son of John, do you love me more than the other disciples do?"

Peter answered him, "Yes, Lord, you know that I love you."

Jesus told him, "Feed my lambs."

[16] Jesus asked him again, a second time, "Simon, son of John, do you love me?"

Peter answered him, "Yes, Lord, you know that I love you."

Jesus told him, "Take care of my sheep."

[17] Jesus asked him a third time, "Simon, son of John, do you love me?"

Peter felt sad because Jesus had asked him a third time, "Do you love me?" So Peter said to him, "Lord, you know everything. You know that I love you."

Jesus told him, "Feed my sheep. [18] I can guarantee this truth: When you were young, you would get ready to go where you wanted. But when you're old, you will stretch out your hands, and someone else will get you ready to take you where you don't want to go." [19] Jesus said this to show by what kind of death Peter would bring glory to God. After saying this, Jesus told Peter, "Follow me!"

[20] Peter turned around and saw the disciple whom Jesus loved. That disciple was following them. He was the one who leaned against Jesus' chest at the supper and asked, "Lord, who is going to betray you?" [21] When Peter saw him, he asked Jesus, "Lord, what about him?"

[22] Jesus said to Peter, "If I want him to live until I come again, how does that concern you? Follow me!" [23] So a rumor that that disciple wouldn't die spread among Jesus' followers. But Jesus didn't say that he wouldn't die. What

Jesus said was, "If I want him to live until I come again, how does that concern you?"

[24] This disciple was an eyewitness of these things and wrote them down. We know that what he says is true.

[25] Jesus also did many other things. If every one of them were written down, I suppose the world wouldn't have enough room for the books that would be written.

A Guide To
REAL HOPE

	Reference	**Page**
ENCOURAGEMENT *When fearful*	John 14:27	46
ENCOURAGEMENT *When afraid of death*	John 3:16 John 10:27-28 John 11:25-27	7 33 35
ENCOURAGEMENT *When discouraged or When facing difficult times*	John 16:33	51
FAITH IN GOD *The benefits*	John 3:16 John 3:36 John 5:24 John 6:40 John 6:47 John 8:31-32,36 John 12:46 John 14:1-3 John 14:12-14 John 20:29-31	7 9 14 18 19 26 41 44 45 62
GOD'S LOVE	John 3:16, 17 John 17:22-26	7 52

	Reference	Page
GOD'S PROMISE OF ETERNAL LIFE	John 3:16	7
	John 3:36	9
	John 5:24	14
	John 6:40	18
	John 6:47	19
	John 6:68-69	20
	John 8:31-32, 36	26
	John 10:27-28	33
	John 11:25-27	35
	John 17:1-3	51
GOD'S WORD	John 5:46	15
	John 17:17	52
	John 20:30-31	62
JOY AND HAPPINESS	John 15:11	47
OBEYING GOD	John 8:31	26
	John 14:15	45
	John 15:10	47
PEACE	John 14:27	46
	John 16:33	50
PRAYING TO GOD *Why and how*	John 15:7	47
	John 16:23-24	50

REAL HOPE
and Prayer

Prayer and the word of God are inseparable—they go together. In his word, God speaks to you. In prayer, you speak to God.

Renew your strength each day by reading God's word and praying according to his will. The following passages will provide you with guidance and *real hope*.

[Jesus began to teach]

"When you pray, go to your room and close the door. Pray privately to your Father who is with you. Your Father sees what you do in private. He will reward you.

"When you pray, don't ramble like heathens who think they'll be heard if they talk a lot. Don't be like them. Your Father knows what you need before you ask him.

"This is how you should pray:

Our Father in heaven,
    let your name be kept holy.
    Let your kingdom come.
    Let your will be done on earth
        as it is done in heaven.
    Give us our daily bread today.
    Forgive us as we forgive others.
    Don't allow us to be tempted.
    Instead, rescue us from the evil one.

Matthew 6:6-13

"That's why I tell you to have faith that you have already received whatever you pray for, and it will be yours. Whenever you pray, forgive anything you have against anyone. Then your father in heaven will forgive your failures."
Mark 11:24-25

If you live in me and what I say lives in you, then ask for anything you want, and it will be yours.
John 15:7

I can guarantee this truth: If you ask the Father for anything in my name, he will give it to you. So far you haven't asked for anything in my name. Ask and you will receive so that you can be completely happy.
John 16:23-24

Be happy in your confidence, be patient in trouble, and pray continually.
Romans 12:12

If any of you are having trouble, pray. If you are happy, sing psalms.
James 5:13

Dear friends, use your most holy faith to grow. Pray with the Holy Spirit's help.
Jude 1:20

REAL HOPE
in the Psalms

At the center of the Bible is the book of Psalms. In them, the whole range of human experience is revealed. David and the other writers praise God, confess their sins, express their doubts and fears, and ask God for help in times of trouble.

Men and women throughout history have come again and again to the book of Psalms for *real hope* and comfort. With the psalmists, they have risen from the depths of despair to the heights of joy as they discovered the power of God's eternal love and faithfulness.

Let this special selection of Psalms guide you into a more secure relationship with your Lord.

Remember, you can trust his promises to rescue, protect, and save you!

That's *real hope!*

PSALM 24

Everything belongs to the LORD. Trust him!

A psalm by David.

1 The earth and everything it contains are the LORD'S.
  The world and all who live in it are his.
2   He laid its foundation on the seas
    and set it firmly on the rivers.

3 Who may go up the LORD's mountain?
  Who may stand in his holy place?
4   The one who has clean hands and a pure heart
    and does not long for what is false
    or lie when he is under oath.
5   This person will receive a blessing from the LORD
    and righteousness from God, his savior.
6 This is the person who seeks him,
    who searchs for the face of the God of Jacob.   *Selah*

7 Lift your heads, you gates.
  Be lifted, you ancient doors,
    so that the king of glory may come in!

8 Who is this king of glory?
    The LORD, strong and mighty!
    The LORD, heroic in battle!

9 Lift your heads, you gates.
  Be lifted, you ancient doors,
    so that the king of glory may come in!

10 Who, then, is this king of glory?
   The LORD of Armies is the king of glory!   *Selah*

PSALM 42

*A prayer to reflect on God's love and kindness
when you feel lonely or discouraged.*

For the choir director; a maskil by Korah's descendants.

1 As a deer longs for flowing streams,
   so my soul longs for you, O God.
2 My soul thirsts for God, for the living God.
   When may I come to see God's face?
3 My tears are my food day and night.
   People ask me all day long, "Where is your God?"
4 I will remember these things as I pour out my soul:
   how I used to walk with the crowd
      and lead it in a procession to God's house.
      I sang songs of joy and thanksgiving
         while crowds of people celebrated a festival.

5   Why are you discouraged, my soul?
     Why are you so restless?
       Put your hope in God,
         because I will still praise him.
         He is my Savior and my God.

6 My soul is discouraged.
   That is why I will remember you
      in the land of Jordon, on the peaks of Hermon, on Mount Mizar.
7 One deep sea calls to another at the roar of your waterspouts.
   All the whitecaps on your waves have swept over me.
8 The LORD commands his mercy during the day,
   and at night his song is with me—
      a prayer to the God of my life.
9   I will ask God, my rock,
      "Why have you forgotten me?
      Why must I walk around mourning
         while the enemy oppresses me?"
10   With a shattering blow to my bones,
      my enemies taunt me.
         They ask me all day long, "Where is your God?"

11   Why are you discouraged, my soul?
     Why are you so restless?
       Put your hope in God,
         because I will still praise him.
         He is my Savior and my God.

PSALM 57

A prayer for help and mercy in times of trouble.

For the choir director; *al tashcheth*; a *miktam* by David when he fled from Saul into the cave.

1 Have pity on me, O God, have pity on me,
    Because my soul takes refuge in you.
        I will take refuge in the shadow of your wings
            until destructive storms pass by.

2 I call to God Most High,
    to the God who does everything for me.
3 He sends his help from heaven and saves me.
    He disgraces the one who is harassing me.   *Selah*
    God sends his mercy and his truth!
4 My soul is surrounded by lions.
    I must lie down with man-eating lions.
        Their teeth are spears and arrows.
        Their tongues are sharp swords.
5   May you be honored above the heavens, O God!
        Let your glory extend over the whole earth!

6 My enemies spread out a net to catch me.
    (My soul is bowed down.)
    They dug a pit to trap me,
        but then they fell into it.   *Selah*

7 My heart is confident, O God,
    my heart is confident!
    I want to sing and make music.
8   Wake up, my soul!
        Wake up, harp and lyre!
    I want to wake up at dawn.
9 I want to give thanks to you among the people, O Lord.
    I want to make music to praise you among the nations
10   because your mercy is as high as the heavens.
        Your truth reaches to the skies.

11   May you be honored above the heavens, O God!
        Let your glory extend over the whole earth!

PSALM 61

A prayer for security and assurance.

For the choir director; on a stringed instrument; by David
1 Listen to my cry for help, O God.
 Pay attention to my prayer.
2 From the ends of the earth, I call to you
   when I begin to lose heart.
 Lead me to the rock that is high above me.
3 You have been my refuge,
   a tower of strength against the enemy.
4 I would like to be a guest in your tent forever
  and to take refuge under the protection of your wings. *Selah*
5 O God, you have heard my vows.
    You have given me the inheritance
     that belongs to those who fear your name.
6 Add days upon days to the life of the king.
 May his years endure throughout every generation.
7 May he sit enthroned in the presence of God forever.
 May mercy and truth protect him.
8 Then I will make music to praise your name forever,
   as I keep my vows day after day.

PSALM 70

An urgent prayer for help!

For the choir director; by David; to be kept in mind.

1 Come quickly to rescue me, O God!
Come quickly to help me, O Lord!
2 Let those who seek my life
   be confused and put to shame.
Let those who want my downfall
   be turned back and disgraced.
3 Let those who say, "Aha! Aha!"
   be turned back because of their own shame.
4 Let all who seek you rejoice and be glad because of you.
Let those who love your salvation continually say,
   "God is great!"

5 But I am oppressed and in need.
O God, come to me quickly.
   You are my help and my Savior.
     O LORD, do not delay!

PSALM 100

The LORD's faithfulness endures forever.

A psalm of thanksgiving.

1 Shout happily to the LORD, all the earth.
2 Serve the LORD cheerfully.
Come into his presence with a joyful song.
3 Realize that the LORD alone is God.
   He made us, and we are his.
   We are his people and the sheep in his care.
4 Enter his gates with a song of thanksgiving.
Come into his courtyards with a song of praise.
Give thanks to him; praise his name.
5 The LORD is good.
   His mercy endures forever.
   His faithfulness endures throughout every generation.

PSALM 117

Praise the LORD for his mercy and faithfulness!

1 Praise the LORD, all you nations!
 Praise him, all you people of the world!
2 His mercy toward us is powerful.
 The LORD's faithfulness endures forever.

Hallelujah!

PSALM 121

You can depend on the LORD for help.

A song for going up to worship.
1 I look up toward the mountains.
 Where can I find help?
2 My help comes from the LORD,
 the maker of heaven and earth.
3 He will not let you fall.
 Your guardian will not fall asleep.
4 Indeed, the Guardian of Israel never rests or sleeps.
5 The LORD is your guardian.
 The LORD is the shade over your right hand.
6 The sun will not beat down on you during the day,
 nor will the moon at night.
7 The LORD guards you from every evil.
 He guards your life.
8 The LORD guards you as you come and go,
 now and forever.

PSALM 130

A prayer for mercy.

A song for going up to worship.

1 O LORD, out of the depths I call to you.
2 O Lord, hear my voice.
   Let your ears be open to my pleas for mercy.
3 O LORD, who would be able to stand
   if you kept a record of sins?
4 But with you there is forgiveness
   so that you can be feared.
5 I wait for the LORD, my soul waits,
   and with hope I wait for his word.
6 My soul waits for the LORD
   more than those who watch for the morning.
   more than those who watch for the morning.
7 O Israel, put your hope in the LORD,
   because with the LORD there is mercy
     and with him there is unlimited forgiveness.
8   He will rescue Israel from all its sins.

PSALM 146

The LORD's help is lasting and complete!

1 Hallelujah!

   Praise the Lord, my soul!
2 I want to praise the LORD throughout my life.
   I want to make music to praise my God as long as I live.

3 Do not trust influencial people,
    mortals who cannot help you.
4   When they breathe their last breath, they return to the ground.
     On that day their plans come to an end.
5 Blessed are those who receive help from the God of Jacob.
    Their hope rests on the LORD their God,
6   who made heaven, earth,
     the sea, and everything in them.
   The LORD remains faithful forever.
7   He brings about justice for those who are oppressed.
   He gives food to those who are hungry.
   The LORD sets prisoners free.
8 The LORD gives sight to blind people.
   The LORD straightens the backs of those who are bent over.
   The LORD loves righteous people.
9 The LORD protects foreigners.
   The LORD gives relief to orphans and widows.
    But he keeps wicked people from reaching their goal.
10 The LORD rules as king forever.
   Zion, your God rules throughout every generation.

   Hallelujah!

About God's Word to the Nations Bible Society

The mission of God's Word to the Nations Bible Society is to make Christ's life-saving, life-changing message more understandable to the 1.1 billion men, women, and children of the world—inside and outside the church, young and old, educated and less educated—who speak English, as well as to hundreds of millions of others who want to learn English.

God's Word to the Nations Bible Society was founded in 1985 as a not-for-profit, tax-exempt 501(c)(3) religious/research organization. The Bible Society managed and funded the translation of GOD'S WORD. This new translation is faithful to the original meaning of the Hebrew, Aramaic, and Greek languages through which God spoke to his people in earlier days, and speaks in clear, natural English to his people today. Its single-column, open layout makes it especially easy to read and understand.

The Bible Society promotes the use of the Scriptures by publishing low-cost (or *free*, if funds are available) versions of GOD'S WORD for distribution to individuals, congregations, mission groups, and other religious organizations worldwide.

For more information, write to

    Executive Director
    God's Word to the Nations Bible Society
    P.O. Box 26343
    Cleveland, OH 44126